Rebecca's Soliloquy

A True Story

Roberta Nee Adams

Copyright © 2014 Roberta Nee Adams.

Art Credit: Sharon Nee Goodman

All rights reserved. No part of this book may be used or reproduced by any means, graphic, electronic, or mechanical, including photocopying, recording, taping or by any information storage retrieval system without the written permission of the publisher except in the case of brief quotations embodied in critical articles and reviews.

LifeRich Publishing is a registered trademark of
The Reader's Digest Association, Inc.

LifeRich Publishing books may be ordered through booksellers or by contacting:

LifeRich Publishing
1663 Liberty Drive
Bloomington, IN 47403
www.liferichpublishing.com
1 (888) 238-8637

Because of the dynamic nature of the Internet, any web addresses or links contained in this book may have changed since publication and may no longer be valid. The views expressed in this work are solely those of the author and do not necessarily reflect the views of the publisher, and the publisher hereby disclaims any responsibility for them.

Any people depicted in stock imagery provided by Thinkstock are models, and such images are being used for illustrative purposes only.

Certain stock imagery © Thinkstock.

ISBN: 978-1-4897-0228-9 (sc)
ISBN: 978-1-4897-0230-2 (hc)
ISBN: 978-1-4897-0229-6 (e)

Library of Congress Control Number: 2014943989

Printed in the United States of America.

LifeRich Publishing rev. date: 08/05/14

To my large and wonderful family, all of whom have made some contribution to my understanding of unconditional love. Related by blood and otherwise, older and younger, near and far, past and present, the connections are there. I appreciate them all. Without you, I could not have written this story. I love you and I like you, too!

A nod to Keith and Jim. One convinced me to get started; the other gave me a deadline. That made the concept a reality for me.

Finally, a special thanks to Sharon Nee Goodman, my sister and co-conspirator on the final project. That was fun!

RNA

In memory of
Alma Nelle Moffatt Rynearson

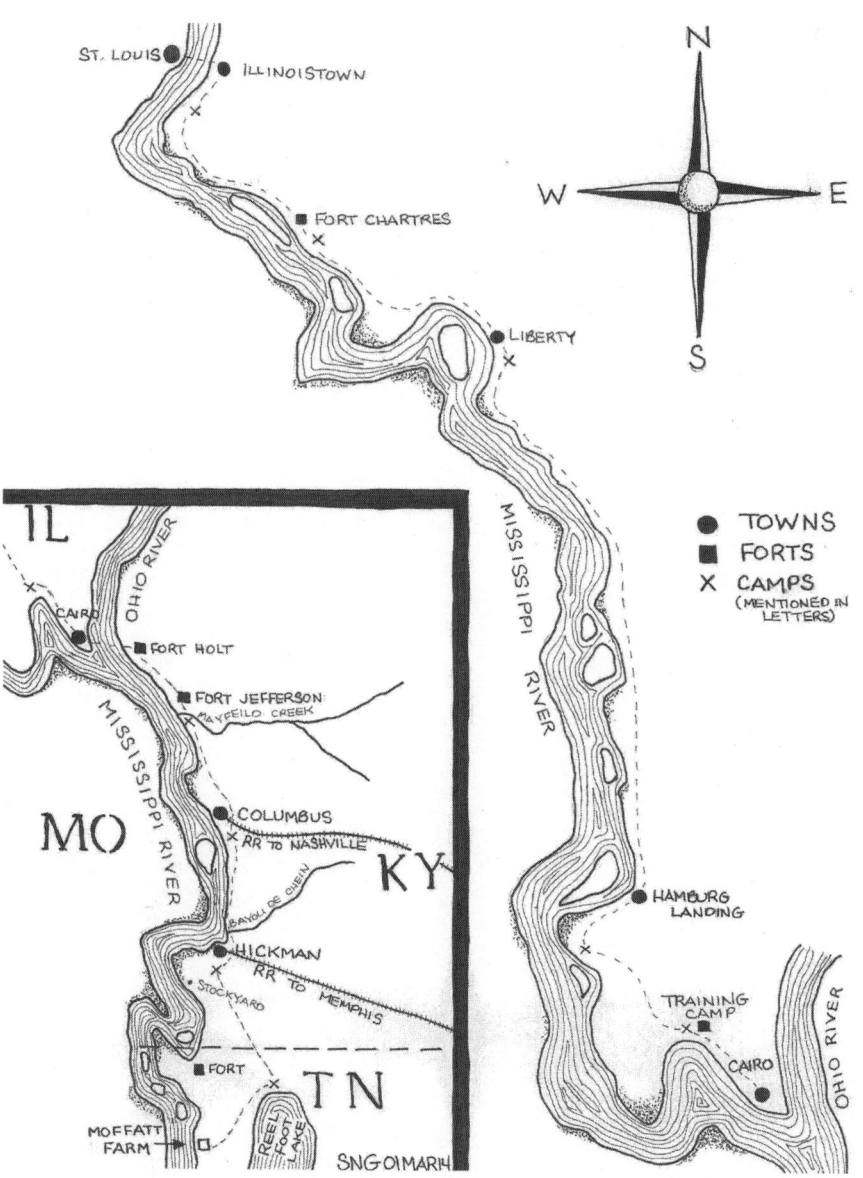

The car slowed, then turned onto the long dirt lane and made its way toward the house that sat proud and stately on the rise. The old woman watched from her rocker on the porch, smiling faintly. She noticed there was no dust trail behind the car. That was good in the springtime. It meant that there was plenty of moisture in the soil, which would be good for the garden. Whether there would be a garden this year, however, was questionable, and it saddened her. She focused again on the car through the indistinct green haze of new buds on the trees, her smile returning.

The car finally pulled up to a stop on the circle drive in front of the porch. A young woman got out and walked around behind the car, grinning up at the old woman on the porch. Stopping in front of the porch she dropped her head back, and spreading out her arms, took an exaggerated deep breath.

"I love it here in the springtime!" she exclaimed. "Just look at those dogwoods, the redbuds! And the daffodils! So beautiful!" Turning in a slow circle she took in the view. "The river doesn't even look so muddy from here!"

Laughing, the girl almost ran up the steps and gave the old woman a hug and kiss before landing in the rocker next to hers.

"But it sure is a bitch in the winter with the ice and snow! So how are you doing, Gramma? All this warm weather must be a lot easier on the arthritis."

"It is," the old woman answered, "I'm always glad to see spring. How about yourself, Sweetie?"

"Oh, fine. You know, about the same as always." The girl hesitated, a little subdued now, and asked, "So. Started any packing yet?"

"It's coming along. There's not really so much, it's only me. Most of the furniture is staying with the house, you know."

"About ready for the big move then, huh?"

"Sure. You know how I miss big city life," the old woman said dryly.

They laughed.

"Yeah, right!" the girl answered. "Hmmm. Memphis. Well, at least your apartment is separate from the house. Plenty of room for a garden. I was down last weekend and Mom has the place almost ready. Have you talked to her?"

The old woman knew that the girl was trying hard to make them both feel better. She had always been the sensitive one, the old woman's favorite.

"Oh, yes. I'm sure she's done a wonderful job. It'll suit me just fine." The old woman quietly sighed, thinking about her years in the big, old house. Good ones, all in all, happy and peaceful years. Her late husband had bought the farm, a gentleman's hobby, and loved the place. She did, too. When he died she had stayed on, though much of the joy was gone from her life. As it does, the passage of time had wrought its changes and finally she could no longer ignore them. Though she had closed off the south wing after his death even half the house was too much for her now and she knew it. It was time to prepare for the last stage of her life. But how she would miss the place! "I'd rather get kicked in the ass with a frozen boot than to have to move, that's all."

"God, Gramma! You and your sayings!" the girl chuckled. She rocked quietly in the comfortable silence, absorbed in her own nostalgic thoughts. She remembered fondly the summers she spent with her grandparents as she grew up. Arriving a few days after school let out, it seemed there was an endless parade of warm, sunny days ahead, full of untold adventure.

She remembered how funny she looked painted in pink calamine lotion the summer she got poison ivy, but didn't remember how miserably she must have itched and how much she must have whined about it. She remembered the hours she spent in the barn loft playing out scenes to imaginary lives she lived, but didn't remember how much it must have hurt the time she jumped out and sprained her ankle when she missed the better part of the haystack below. She remembered roaming around the countryside, playing in the river, helping in the garden. She thought of the nights she would slip out of bed and sit by her open window, watching the moon over the river, and listening to the whippoorwills call to each other from the fencerows over the constant chirp of crickets. Forgotten were the bug bites, the sunburn, various scratches and occasional stitches. She remembered her grandparents' smiles.

Suddenly it would be over. Time to pack and go home, the bittersweet feeling tempered with the excitement of starting another school year. And always there was the promise of next summer.

Now it felt to her as if the rock solid foundations of her

childhood were eroding with time, starting to crumble. She was beginning to understand how tenuous the connections in life, how precious.

"Remember Janice down the road? I went to Vacation Bible School with her every summer at the Baptist church past her house." The girl chuckled softly. "I was going to be a missionary and she was going to be a schoolteacher. We must have talked about everything in the world. And the letters we'd write during the school years! Pages and pages! So serious and so silly. Best friends."

"Still miss her, don't you?" the old lady asked gently. "I know, I lost my best friend, too. Most women don't think of their husbands that way. I was lucky."

"So what do you do, Gramma? What do you do..." the girl asked, almost to herself.

"The best you can, Sweetie, there's no replacing them. We can remember the good things. And we can be thankful we had them." The old woman closed her eyes and reached over to pat the girl's hand; sorry she had no better answer.

"Yeah. I just miss her so much," the girl said wistfully. "Well, I found my husband here, too, so that's something." She brightened a little.

The old lady smiled. "Yes, and he's a good boy, I like him. I see he got the promotion, I saw his picture in the paper."

"How about that? Superintendent of schools. Not too bad, huh? Except that now he's not just my husband, he's my boss, too!" The girl rolled her eyes. "You can imagine how that plays at home!" They laughed again. "Oh, he'll be out for dinner after the board meeting."

"Good. Well, tell me. Have you two discussed my offer?

I'll need to call Jake pretty soon if I'm going to have him turn the garden for you."

"Yes, Gramma. We've discussed it. I don't know yet. I mean, you know how much I love this place, and he does, too. And he's really quite the handyman. He loves puttering around as much as Gramps did. He just doesn't want to live so far out of town. We haven't decided against it, it's just he's not real enthusiastic..." her voice trailed off.

"Like it's that far a drive. Honestly, he's a good boy, but he could loosen up a little," the old woman muttered.

"Gramma! I don't believe you just said that! Okay, it may be true, he should," the girl admitted with a grin. "Seriously, he always talks about how relaxing it is out here. You have room to stretch. Great for kids. And it's so pretty. It's just the drive he doesn't like."

"So how far is it, anyway?"

"Oh, about eighteen miles to our house. But I guess it's maybe fourteen miles to the administration building from here."

"That's not so far. Hardly any traffic, anyway."

"True. And actually it'd be closer for me. I don't think my school is more than five or six miles from here." The girl leaned back in the rocker, sighing. "I do love old houses, you know, especially this one. I like its personality. Old houses have such character. It's almost like they have their own quiet lives that encompass all of the people that have ever lived in them. Too bad they can't talk," she said as if to herself.

The girl rocked, lost in her own thoughts for a few moments. Finally realizing she hadn't heard a response she glanced over to the old woman, only to find her looking back, smiling.

"What?" she asked defensively. "I think they do have character and personality. I mean, you told me this house was standing before the Civil War. Can't you just imagine?"

"Yes, and I happen to agree with you about the house, Sweetie. I've always felt the same way. I've always thought this was a strong, happy house. At peace with itself. It's just odd that you should mention it talking." The old lady still smiled.

"Uh-oh. Don't tell me it speaks to you at night; you hear funny voices or anything," the girl warned, sitting up straight.

"Not hardly. But before you decide for sure on my offer I want you to read something."

"Okay, you had me worried there for a minute. What is it?"

The old woman reached into her apron pocket, pulled out an envelope and handed it to the girl.

"A letter."

It was very old; the girl could see that immediately. There was only a single name written in flowing script on the outside, Augustus. She looked up at the old woman with a puzzled expression. The old woman just smiled and nodded for her to continue. The girl took the letter from the old woman, slipped it out of the envelope, carefully unfolded it, and began to read...

My Darling Augustus,   *18 July 1864*

I awoke again this morning a little after two and with my coverlet slipped out onto the porch and sat in my rocker next to yours. If I rest my hand on the arm of yours it rocks with mine. I close my eyes and listen to them rocking together and I imagine you there with me, talking like you used to of the day's events, or plans and dreams; or reading to me the beautiful poems and stories.

I remember the time we danced in the moonlight while you sang to me, soft and clear. With your arms around me I rested my head on your chest and it felt so precious. It was as if those few moments were predestined for us, and we stepped into them and lived them perfectly. Nothing else existed for that short time. When you took me to bed that night you loved me as you never had before, and I felt the intensity as I never had before. That is the memory burned into my heart more brightly than any other. Did we sense then what was coming? You've been gone so long now, Augustus, and I don't know where you are or what has happened to you. Will you come back to me? And if you do, will we have been changed too much, gone too far past those moments to feel the same way? Questions for which I have no answers. Sometimes I despair ever feeling such joy again and if that is true, so be it. At least we had those moments, that love, and we knew it. We lived it. If we do someday find that moment again, or another, then we will be the fortunate ones.

I rock and I doze, ever aware of the night sounds around me, knowing they portend no danger. As the sky begins to lighten I look down toward the river and see the mist. It is as if the river sleeps, and in her dreams rises ghostlike from her banks and wanders freely to those places she cannot go in waking. As daylight finally overtakes the night I go back up to my room, seat myself at my desk, take up my pen and write to you again.

There is still the farm, my dear Augustus, your life and your blood, to carry me through. I know that we have fared better here than many. Since last week the only slaves left with us are Joseph and Belle, Samson and Lizbeth, and the brothers Jonas and Joshua and their families. The others have left in ones or twos or families, seeking peace and freedom. Those who have stayed have done so by choice as well. We do what we can, Darling, but the fields lie fallow now, except the west field where we had planted yams and corn. The Yankees took most of the crop. They burned our landing on the river. The fences have been torn down, the barns are in need of paint and repair and the house as well, but they still stand. Only yesterday a Yankee patrol was here and took our last hog and what few guineas they could catch. They must have all been city boys; they made quite a picture trying to chase them down. They had to work for that supper. Samson keeps Daisy hidden in the swamp or the Yankees would have her. So we have milk for the children. We still have old Rusty to plow the garden and pull the dogcart. I suppose even the Yankees could tell that neither would be of much use to them.

I've lost count of the how many times the soldiers have been here, our boys too, Augustus, picking the farm over like blue and gray vultures. I think that is what has shaken me worst of all, that there doesn't seem to be any difference. They all act as if they are entitled to whatever we may have that they want and we are powerless to stop any of them. Gone are the wagons and the horses, the stock, even the silver and crystal. At least they are fewer of late. After all this time they must finally realize the futility of searching for anything of value here.

I have managed to keep the garden, Darling, a fine one. I've planted all of your favorites, and with so few of us here we usually have enough to eat and some to share with Alma and the children. And though the soldiers often help themselves to whatever is available, they haven't destroyed it. It is the only thing that gives me hope and faith these days, my dear. It is the only thing that is the same as it was before the war. It has the same rhythm, takes the same care, and bears the same fruits of my labors as it always has. The sun rises as it did before, but now I fear what the day will bring. My heart beats as it did before, but now I am not sure as to what purpose. Only my garden, Augustus, is the same.

I've even managed to keep my flowers though I was told I was a fool for doing so. It's the only beauty I see these days. I have my hollyhocks and peonies, zinnias, asters, marigolds and nasturtium. Morning glories have come up by the side porch and I have left them alone. On their own they have flourished. How many times I have heard you curse them! And I imagine I have pulled as many as you have. But I have come to admire them, Augustus. They are survivors. Through the coldest winters, the hottest summers, flood and drought, they live on and bloom. Beautiful, fragile blooms that you can only see for a short time each morning. Sometimes I feel like one of them, clinging *to whatever I can to keep going, living for the few beautiful moments. And we will have our beautiful moments again, my love, as sure as those morning glories will bloom again. I believe it. I must believe it.*

Ever yours,
Rebecca

When she finished reading the girl was silent for a few moments.

"Gramma, wherever did you get this?" she whispered. "Who are these people?"

"Come here. I'll show you." the woman answered, her eyes twinkling.

The old woman rose and went into the house, the girl close on her heels. They went into the front parlor and the woman crossed the room to the fireplace on the far wall. It was a large working fireplace framed by an oak mantel with carved columns that reached to the ceiling. The years had darkened the finish to the color of honey. Ornate green and white tiles were set into the space between the fireplace opening and the mantel crosspiece. A large mirror framed with the same green tile was set above the crosspiece between the columns. The crosspiece itself was made of dark green marble and extended through the columns on either side with the sides and front of the crosspiece was carved into receding layers. Resting her hand on the right side of the crosspiece, the old woman turned back to the girl.

"This is my favorite room, you know. I do most of my reading here." The old woman smiled. "You know I have the fireplace cleaned every fall, I use it a lot. Well, last fall I finally replaced the mantel crosspiece. You remember the big crack in it, don't you? I'd been meaning to do it for the longest. Cost me a bundle, too, I had to have it custom made. Anyway, the workman found this..."

The old woman moved her hand to the paneling above and to the side of the crosspiece. She pressed against the wood and then took her hand away. Slowly a small hidden door swung open to reveal a secret compartment. Inside were stacks of letters tied into bundles with light blue ribbon.

"There's another one on this side." She moved to the other side of the fireplace and pressed again on the paneling. Another door swung open to reveal an identical compartment, also filled with letters. Reaching into this one, she took out a small leather bound hinged frame. She opened it and looked down at it for a moment before handing it to the girl.

The girl stared, her eyes wide, mouth slightly open.

"Oh my god. This is them. Isn't it? You mean they actually lived here? Right in this house? I've got goose bumps! There must be a hundred letters there! Are they all hers? She's so pretty. He – god, he looks severe in that uniform – but nice looking." The girl looked back up at the woman, waiting to hear more.

"There are a hundred and four letters all together. I spent most of the winter sorting through them, reading them and putting them in order. They tell quite a story."

The old woman took out three bundles and closed the doors.

"I've picked these out. I want you to read them. You have all afternoon. It's a beautiful day, go sit out on the porch. I'll make you a sandwich and some tea in a little bit."

The girl stretched out her hands and took the letters without another word, holding them as if they might break. Slowly she walked out to the porch, settled herself into a rocker and began to read.

Dearest Augustus,   22 July 1864

    A little break from my normal routine today, Darling. I visited Alma and the children in town. They fare well, both children having mercifully recovered from chicken pox. Little Charles is six now and you would know him anywhere, Augustus, he is the image of your dear brother. He has the same sandy hair and blue eyes, the same open face and endearing grin. He's a darling boy, friendly and considerate, though quite capable of a boy's mischief, the little man of the house in your brother's absence. He absolutely dotes on little Althea. She's four now and a beautiful child with features more like her mother with her chestnut hair, large brown eyes, and fair skin. She's quieter that Charles is but very sweet and loving. She adores him as much as he does her. I've never seen a brother and sister any closer.

    As I do every visit I tried again to coax Alma to bring the children and stay here, but she will not hear of leaving her home in town. I worry about her there in town with only Mattie and the children. When I argue that it is not safe for her with no man there she points out that there are many women now who have no man with them, and will never have them back as she and I will. I envy her optimism in these times but it does not diminish my anxiety. Neither for her nor myself. So I visit as often as I can and do what I am able to help. She has tried so hard to be brave and strong. And she has managed the children wonderfully. Charles has only vague memories of his father and, of course, Althea none at all. So Alma tells them stories of him and shows them his picture every day. I love her for it. And I can tell you, Augustus, she can embellish a story! As if any stories of Charles need to be embellished, he's so boisterous and fun loving.

I know that you are not most fond of her, Dear, but we have become so close with you and Charles gone. She was raised differently than we, an only child, a town girl, and she feels it. With Charles being so outgoing we just never really got to know Alma well. She's not spoiled at all, just quiet and rather shy. I'm proud of how well she has coped with only Mattie left there to help her. You would be proud of her, too.

This spring I even helped her put in a small garden behind the house. You would have split your sides laughing at us, covered in dirt and laughing so much at ourselves that we couldn't keep our rows straight! Even the children had fun helping with it, picking stones out of the plot. And the little garden has served them well.

We have discovered that Alma has quite a flair for designing clothes. Though not the priority it once was, she has two growing children to clothe. She has taken many a garment apart to fashion it into another. Her designs are both imaginative and tasteful while being thrifty with our fabric at the same time. We haven't worn hoops in some time now, and Augustus, I can hardly say I miss them!

I have taken over a good deal of the sewing myself. Charles bought Alma a treadle sewing machine before the war, and though she never admitted it to him, she is petrified of it! Lucy always did the sewing, but she has long since left. So I have learned to use it. It is quite fun actually; it is amazingly fast and sews beautifully even stitches.

As much as I have helped her, Augustus, she has been a godsend to me, a true friend. We talk about almost everything. We gossip and giggle like schoolgirls while we do our sewing; we discuss the children and their difficulties seriously like grown, mature women; and we reminisce about you and Charles and the days before the war like two old biddies. She has held me up when I've felt I could no longer stand on my own, and I have done the same for her. We lean on each other, laugh together and cry together. We keep each other going.

You and I still have the farm, Augustus, but the Yankees looted and burned Charles store long ago and even confiscated his bank account. They have only the house left yet Alma remains hopeful and brave. Knowing what she has been through I feel ashamed that I feel so sorry for myself sometimes. Why is it that this war utterly destroys some people while it tempers others into finer, stronger people? Not only on the battlefields and in the camps, but all the way back home to those left there. I haven't an answer, but I do believe that there are more heroes in this war than just those men who fight it.

Good night, Darling,
Rebecca

My Love,   28 July 1864

    Some good news today, Mary and little Shane have come to stay. They arrived only yesterday. But it's a sad occasion, too, Augustus, with her so recently having lost Phillip. Hardly two years married and now she's a widow with a small baby and not yet twenty years old. How very unfair! He wasn't even fighting, he was returning from a business trip to New Orleans, trying to save his father's brokerage, when the steamboat, a civilian boat, was shelled by Yankees. She and Phillip were so happy and their future seemed so bright. He was an industrious young man with such promise. Like so many we have lost. I don't know anyone who deserved happiness more, Mary has always been so concerned with everyone else's happiness. Now hers is gone.

    The trip from Memphis was difficult for them. Traveling on the river now is so dangerous. The boat was hardly more than a skiff. There was no one to help her with her baggage, what little she brought, and no food. They traveled through the night, sleeping on crates stacked at the back of the boat. Somehow one of her cases was lost, evidently having fallen overboard at some point. And, Augustus, she paid their passage with Phillip's gold pocket watch! As if she's not in enough pain, I can imagine how it must have hurt her to part with it. It should have gone to little Shane so he would at least have something of his father's. Silly and useless for us to fret over such things, but they pain none the less.

    I am worried about her, Darling. I don't know how she made it here on her own. She seems so overwhelmed; I think she is still in shock. She can barely attend to the baby and she hardly relates to anything around her. It's like she's gone deep inside herself, closed herself off from the rest of the world. Since we were children she has always had such a sunny, outgoing disposition. Even when she was troubled she never let it show and would only rarely speak of it. I can only imagine that this pain must be more than she can bear. I am glad she has come here. This will be her home now, and she'll be with people who know her and love her. We'll do all that we can to help her heal and I'm sure that little Shane will help pull her through, too. But I wonder, Augustus, how well any of us will heal from the wounds that this war has inflicted on us, both seen and unseen.

Even little Shane, only nine months old, seems affected by it all. He is very quiet and rarely fusses. He watches us all closely, especially Mary. I have not yet seen him smile or heard him laugh, but I hope that he will soon feel secure enough with us to do so. He is such a beautiful baby, Augustus, with big dark eyes and dark hair. Bell and Lizbeth have taken to him so that Mary and I hardly have an opportunity to touch him! He will hardly be lacking in attention and care. And love.

Jonas and Joshua and their families have left us, two days ago, headed north to a new life. I gave them their papers as I have all of the others, just as you instructed me before you left. But I worry about them, too. Every slave on our farm was born into slavery just as you and I were born into the system. Even though you have always treated our people well I can understand that it can't be right for any human being to own another human being. I can understand their hunger for freedom, for a life of their own choosing. You must have felt the same or you wouldn't have written their papers before you left. But how does one change a whole society and its way of life with the stroke of a pen? Do we just give them their papers, tell them they are free, then turn our backs and believe our hands and conscience are clean? I don't feel it's enough, Augustus, it's not responsible. For all the talk and high ideals I don't think the north has any better idea of how to change it than we do. None of the Yankees I've seen have treated any of the Negros with near the respect you always have, Augustus. Do you think the Yankees consider them free and equal men? I don't see it. How are they going to make their own place in society with so few who will help them or even give them a chance? Are men any less chattel to be used for political gain as to be worked in the fields? The answers lay ahead us yet and I fear will not be easily found.

Joseph and Belle have made it clear that they are staying with their family, as have Samson and Lizbeth. I'm grateful for that as I consider them part of the family as well. I talk to Belle as I imagine I would have my own mother had she lived. She has taught me to cook and I have offered to teach her to read. She just laughs and tells me she is too old for all of that, but she has me read to her sometimes. She misses your reading almost as much as I. For now I am a poor but acceptable substitute. Joseph is as protective and correct as he has always been. I think he has had a harder time than the rest of us. A lot of protocol has fallen casualty to the war, my dear, as surely as has slavery. We have to be practical now. Joseph struggles more to reconcile the way things have become with the ways he feels they should be. My heart goes out to him.

You grew up with Samson, you know how he is! And he has done as well as anyone could with the farm in your absence. He's not worried about the future and talks constantly of bringing the farm back to its former glory when you return. You know how smart he is, Augustus, and he's full of good ideas. He works as hard as any two men, but it is not possible for him to do the work of twenty. Even the fact that there's no one left to help him now doesn't seem to daunt him in the least. I suppose his view that the decline in conditions here is a temporary state helps him to cope. I do not discourage him.

And so we carry on, Darling, trying to find our way through this madness, separately and together. I think so much of you, caught up in the same madness and, I imagine, trying to find your way, too. Will you find your way back to me? You must, Augustus. It is what I live for, and the only thing that makes any sense in all of this, the only thing that could put an end to this madness. Come back to me, Darling.

Your
Rebecca

My Dear,   3 August 1864

I am just returning home after visiting with Alma for a few days. The most wonderful news, Augustus, your brother Charles is home now for good. Sadly, there is no good news these days that is not tainted with tragedy. He has lost his left arm while fighting near Clifton. And, I fear, part of his soul as well.

Old Dr. Gray came to see him and feels that the wound will heal well enough and says that Charles is otherwise in good health, all things considered, though he is quite thin. He showed Alma how to care for and dress the wound and she helped him right along, never acting the least bit faint. Bless her, she is absolutely ecstatic to have him back in any shape.

Alma helped him bathe, washed and cut his hair and shaved him, and gave him some of his old clothes to wear. Darling, he seems almost a ghost of his former self. The clothing hung as if on a scarecrow. But that is not what really concerns me. His demeanor seems quite subdued and preoccupied. I'm so used to his booming voice and joyful laugh. Now the sadness in his smile would break your heart. He speaks neither of the past nor of the future, and appears content with the moment at hand. I think that both may be too overwhelming for him just now. He sometimes stares off at nothing, as if he's hundreds of miles away. Perhaps he is. Occasionally he walks through the house touching things, looking at them as if seeing them for the first time. Surely he has noticed how many are missing now. He appears to be struggling to get his bearings again, to readjust to the old way of life that is nothing like it used to be. How does one do that? Alma and I have lived through the changes day by day but to him it has happened all at once. He left a very prosperous man and returns to find that he is practically a pauper. But it doesn't seem to concern him unduly. I suppose three years of this war prepared him for what he might find when he returned home.

The children were quite shy of him at first. Then finally little Charles could contain himself no longer. He walked right up to Charles and without preamble asked him if it was true that he took him for a ride on a horse the day he was born. I told you that Alma could embellish a story! At first Charles looked surprised and immediately glanced over at Alma. The look on her face must have given her away because he turned back to little Charles and with the utmost sincerity he answered "Yes. And the second day I took you fishing." Since then they have been practically inseparable. Once little Charles warmed up Althea followed. She is in his lap any time he sits, even for meals.

Alma and I took Charles out and showed him the garden. He did laugh at that! And Alma's version of the day we put the garden in had us all in tears of laughter. The children were proud to tell him all about their efforts and they all set to work almost immediately to get it in better shape. The children chatted like magpies and Alma was afraid it would be too much for Charles, but he would not hear of going back into the house and took it all in with almost a smile.

Last night the three of us were sitting in the parlor after the children had gone to bed. Alma and I were talking when she noticed that Charles was just sitting there in his chair, staring at nothing. She rose and crossed the room to him, knelt in front of his chair and took his hand, smiling softly and looking straight into his eyes. Her touch must have brought him back. His eyes met hers and they sat that way without speaking a word, just looking into each other's eyes. Then he squeezed her hand and I saw a tear slide down his cheek. Her smile never wavered; her eyes never left his and his never left hers. They were reconnecting, she was giving him strength, and he was truly coming home. It was one of the most touching, beautiful moments I have ever witnessed, Augustus, it filled my heart. I slipped out of the room and went upstairs to bed.

I can hardly describe how I felt, rejoicing for them, grieving for you. It felt as if I had been kissed on one cheek and slapped on the other. I felt more hopeful that we will find each other again if you come home to me, and more fearful that you may never return. I feel so torn. I feel my nerves fray a little more each day. I slept fitfully and returned home this morning. Charles and Alma no longer need me there. They have found their way back together. I thank God.

So I wait, Augustus, for you to come home. No matter what has passed in your life or mine we can find each other again. I have seen it happen. The human soul is an amazing thing. Above all hopeful, therefore enduring. I still have hope, so I will endure the fear and hardship and I will be here for you when you come home. If you come home.

My love,
Rebecca

Darling Augustus,   7 August 1864

As I write, Dear, it is a little after two in the morning. Again I awoke as I often do now at this same hour when even time seems to sleep. Do I want to hold it here, or do I want to move it on to morning? I don't know. I wake, restless, so I go out on the porch to rock or up into the attic to watch out the west windows.

Tonight it is raining, a slow, steady summer rain with low rumbles of thunder in the distance. In that moment between sleep and consciousness I heard it and thought it was Yankee cannons, and even judged they were too far away to harm us here. Then I smelled the breeze and knew it was only thunder. So I came up to the attic and sit at the windows looking out to the river. I sat all night in this very spot the night the Yankees burned our landing, watching them. I can look down on the west barn from here and I waited to see if they would burn it, too. As close as it is to the house, and full of hay, I knew we would never be able to contain it before it spread.

But the Yankees only burned landings that night. You could see the fires from here, up and down the river. I remembered wondering why they even bothered burning them. There was no one left to harvest and ship the crops that were in, those that they hadn't already stolen or destroyed. Perhaps they were bored and just did it for sport. Who can say? I've long since stopped trying to make any sense out of this war.

I only want it to end. I am tired, Augustus, bone weary. It shames me to say it because I am sure the sacrifices I've made don't begin to compare to the horrors you've endured, but it's true. How can this madness and destruction go on for so long? How much longer can it continue? I can't imagine. Sometimes I can hardly think. We all work so hard just to eat and keep clothes on our backs. How much I took for granted that I have to consider so carefully now! Going to town to purchase whatever material I wanted for dresses, some I wore for only one occasion. The yards and yards of material I bought just for petticoats, Augustus, and those petticoats long gone to bandage bloody Confederate wounds. I used to light as many candles as I wanted without a thought. Why, we burned them by the bushel in just the two chandeliers! Now we are so careful with our candles and lamps that we usually go to bed shortly after dark. And desserts with dinner, sometimes two or three! They are a luxury now we can no longer afford, they take so much sugar and lard.

So many material things that we thought were important, things that we thought would make us happy and secure! And though it's difficult to do without so much, it's not those things that I miss and want back. It's you, Augustus. You are my happiness and security. It's all the pleasures we had together that I miss. The way you used to read to me while I watched the expressions on your face and listened to the inflections of your voice. You made poetry sound like music. How many times did I catch myself holding my breath, fascinated, listening to you? I read now on rare occasions, but it's only to hear the echo of your voice reading those same words.

I miss our walks to the river, the evenings we would sit out on the porch, talking late into the night, the whippoorwills keeping company with us. I miss how sometimes you would come in when I bathed and wash my hair for me. How sweet and delightfully silly you could be, and how we laughed! I miss that intimacy, that connection, that love. I miss the people we become when we are together.

That's what I want back. I can do without the material things, Augustus. It's being without you that rends my soul and tortures me so. The longing and fear haunt me, Darling, like malicious ghosts whom, though unseen, are there; around a corner, behind a door. At night they come out to haunt me. They wake me in a cold sweat at two o'clock in the morning. During the day I can be strong, I have faith, I believe you'll come back to me. But the nights, Augustus, how I dread the nights! That is when my strength abandons me and I feel so alone and afraid.

Where are you and when are you coming back? Three years, Augustus! Are you ever coming home? I don't even know where you are, what has become of you. But surely, I tell myself, had your heart stopped beating then my own would have stopped as well. Would it not? Wouldn't I at least know in my heart if you had been killed? I am afraid, Darling, because I don't know. That is the torture I live with every day, every night. God forgive me, but how I envy Alma, and yes, even Mary. For them the torture is over. Alma has her Charles back, even missing an arm. And

Mary knows that Phillip is never coming back. But the waiting and wondering is over for them. Mine continues to haunt me, so I haunt the house at night like one of my ghosts.

Please come back to me, my Darling. No matter what this war has done to us we'll find each other, heal each other. I can endure anything except losing you. At two o'clock in the morning I need you and I want you here with me. Please, Darling. Soon.

Ever yours,
Rebecca

My Augustus,   10 August 1864

Tonight I put my hand to write you with the greatest trepidation. I must tell you what has happened, what I have done. I fear I cannot adequately express myself to make you see it and feel it as I did, and to make you understand why I reacted as I did. I don't understand myself. It all happened in the blink of an eye, Augustus.

This morning Joseph and Samson brought in some hay from the east fields. When they came up to the west barn to unload it Samson unhitched Rusty from the cart and led her around to the watering trough. I passed him on my way from the house to the barn to speak to Joseph. I wanted to let him know that dinner was ready and unloading the hay could wait, it was so beastly hot.

As I stepped into the barn I heard Joseph in the hay crib and while I crossed to the crib door my eyes were only beginning to adjust to the dimness. The next few seconds passed like an eternity, Augustus. Everything seemed to be magnified, but it seemed to happen so slowly, as if in a dream. Yet at the same time the images met my eye and thoughts crossed my mind so quickly that they hardly registered. Joseph with a pitchfork raised why movement at his feet bloody an animal maybe rabid a hand raised beseeching my God a man my stomach clenches red hair red beard Oh God in Heaven Augustus Augustus heat runs through me like lightening I cannot move I cannot speak I cannot breath pounding in my ears my temples blue why blue uniform he's home Joseph don't kill him now someone screams "No Joseph no!" Blackness.

I awoke to Joseph and Samson patting my face and wrists with water. I called your name and struggled to get to you and they held me back. No, they told me, it wasn't you. I ceased to struggle, but slowly turned my head to look at the man lying within arm's reach of me, unconscious and covered in blood. Your hair, your beard, even the shape of your face. But not you. A blue uniform, a Yankee. I retched, again and again, and before I fainted for the second time in my life, I heard myself whisper, "Don't kill him." Forgive me, my Darling, please forgive me. I don't know why I said it.

It was dark when I woke again and found myself in bed. Belle was there with me and brought me some sassafras tea. She was quite concerned for me after the shock I had sustained but I convinced her that I was well enough and pressed her to tell me what had happened. Joseph found the Yankee in the crib when he went in to stack the old hay before unloading the cart. Afraid we would be blamed for the Yankees wounds if he were found there by a patrol, Joseph did indeed intend to kill him and hide the body. But I walked in at that moment. Of course Samson heard my scream and came running in just as I fainted. Both of them heard me tell them not to kill him before I fainted the second time. Samson carried me to the house and Belle and Lizbeth put me to bed while Joseph and Samson argued about the Yankee. Joseph still wanted to kill him. But Samson prevailed, his strongest argument being that I wanted the Yankee alive for some reason.

All of the commotion even roused Mary from her room. Belle concocted a story of my fainting from the heat and easily dissuaded her offer to help, and the kept her busy and out of harm's way the rest of the afternoon with mending. She knows nothing of the Yankee and need never know. She rarely leaves the house and never goes to the barn. Thank goodness.

Belle and Lizbeth went out to the barn and cleaned the Yankee's wounds, poulticed and bandaged them, and dressed him in some of Samson's clothes. He was in and out of consciousness as they tended him, but did not fight them. Samson burned the uniform. They fashioned a pallet for him there in the barn and Samson and Joseph are taking turns watching him. Belle tells me he has a head wound, and has been shot in the left shoulder and hip. The wounds were not yet infected and weren't of themselves life threatening except that they hadn't been treated and he had lost a lot of blood. Belle feels he will likely recover.

From his effects we know that he is a major with a cavalry unit from Kentucky. His name is Stephen Gardner. He was unarmed and we haven't seen a stray horse anywhere. I haven't the slightest idea how or why he came to our barn.

He is out there still, Augustus, living and breathing, his wounds tended and healing, sleeping on a soft, dry pallet because I allowed it. And I don't know why. I wonder how many men he has caused to die. I wonder if he has ever spared a life he could have taken. It disturbs me so that he looks like you. Where are you tonight, Augustus? Are you dry and comfortable? Are you wounded and hurting? By being merciful to this Yankee am I hoping to purchase you some needed mercy? Perhaps. If I could make such a bargain with the Almighty I would do so. But I am too weary and drained to reason it out tonight, and I've yet to decide what to do about the man in the barn. I dare not even consider what you would think about what I have done. Tomorrow is time enough and I will face it then.

Good night my Dear,
Rebecca

My Dear,   15 August 1864

It has been five days since I last wrote and told you about the Yankee. He is still here with us, recovering in the barn. My mind and my thoughts are still much disturbed for I have not yet made any decision about him. I feel such dread within me for having him here. What if he was found? How could I explain this to Mary, or Charles and Alma, or even you? There is no way that I could. Even now Joseph and Belle, Samson and Lizbeth wonder as to my motives and intentions. They say nothing, but I see the questions in their eyes. And I know they see no answers in mine.

I could easily have Joseph or Samson put him in the cart and take him to town and turn him over to the Yankees. Or I could just tell Joseph to kill him and bury him. This is war, after all, he is the enemy. And who would ever know? Yet in the midst of all of this turmoil in my heart I know I must wait. Perhaps my heart is telling me that there must be a reason that he came to our barn. I have a sense of something in the periphery of my consciousness. Something of which I have no knowledge yet and will not control but in which I will play a part. The morning after we danced on the porch in the moonlight I had the same feeling. I looked at you with different eyes, as if trying to memorize your face, your manner, even your voice. I couldn't touch you enough. We even made love in the middle of the afternoon that day; I couldn't wait to have you that close to me again. Then before the month was out you were gone. War. I realize that none of this makes any rational sense at all. But I feel it so strongly and my intuition tells me to wait. So I shall, for a little while longer at least.

It was not until yesterday that I could bring myself to go to the barn and speak to him. Belle advised against it, but I had to see for myself what kind of person he is. I was torn between hoping that he would be some kind of monster and fearing that he would not be so. If the first proved to be true my decision would be easily made and I could soon put the ordeal behind me. If not, then my decision would be much more difficult.

I found him to be well mannered and quietly spoken, and expressive of his gratitude for my having saved his life. He was reluctant to speak of how he came to our barn and would only say that he was traveling with two escorts north to south along the river when they were ambushed a few miles from here. Both escorts were killed and he was wounded and left for dead. Eventually he managed to get back on his horse and rode a little further south. He was in sight of our barn when he fell off. He walked a little, but mostly crawled the rest of the way. I did not question him further. I do not want to know any more. The only question he asked was why I saved his life. I told him the truth, Augustus, I don't know. Neither of us spoke of what was to become of him. He wears a wedding ring. Somewhere a woman waits for him. Perhaps even children.

He is not a monster; he is a man, far from home, wounded and war-weary. His manner spoke it. I saw none of the righteous indignation or superiority I've seen in other Yankee soldiers. Perhaps he is humbled by receiving aid from the enemy. Perhaps all of the bright, shining rhetoric of before the war has tarnished and he has learned the true meaning of it. What a great disparity between the ideal and the reality! What glory can there be in spilling another man's blood on the battlefield? What triumph is there in taking food from women and children left behind who are already on the threshold of starvation? How very pathetic that we have allowed, indeed encouraged, this to come to pass. That is how I felt after talking to him, Augustus, just disappointed and sick at heart. I couldn't even hate him.

Out of uniform, with the blood cleaned off he doesn't look as much like you as I first thought. He is older, a little thinner, and I think shorter. Even so, he looks enough like you that I find it disturbing. When he turns his head or looks down I can almost see you sitting there. I will not deny that his resemblance to you contributed to my reluctance to kill him and to my indecision. But only in small part. Quite truthfully I wish he had never come here. I don't know that I will speak to him again. I don't know that I can bear it. I only know now that I will not kill him.

I slept restlessly and awoke again this morning a little after two missing you so terribly, Darling. The longing does not diminish with time, it only grows. I got out of bed and went to the wardrobe and found one of your shirts. I slipped off my nightgown and put your shirt on, wrapping it around my nakedness and holding it close, trying to catch the briefest scent of you, remembering the feel of your hands on me. I thought of the way you kiss me, Augustus, the feel of your lips on mine, the caress of your tongue, the way you kiss my neck and I can feel your lips, your beard, and your breath all at once. I think of the feel of your beard, your ears, your shoulder against my lips. I press the back of my hand against my lips to bring the feeling back, I run my fingers down my neck, across my breast, over my body. Gently I stroke my thigh, bringing my fingers up to where I am warm for you.

But it's not your touch, Augustus, you're not here. And I can't touch you, hold your face in my hands, press my lips to yours, run my hands over your muscled body. I remember how you made me feel inside, valued and appreciated, but lusted for as well! No matter what your mood, teasing and playful, urgent and lustful, or tender and giving, you satisfy my soul and body together completely. The way you touch me, the things you whisper to me, you take me to where there is nothing else in this world but to feel you inside me, so hard, filling me so perfectly, the rhythm of your body driving me to such joyful ecstasy that all I want is to give it all back and take you there, too. You make me feel free to express my love in any manner I choose, to show you how I feel. I ache for you, Darling, so terribly that I sometimes think you must feel it no matter where you are. Do you feel it? Do you think of me and remember how it felt making love to me? Is it enough to bring you back? I believe so, Augustus, not only for the act itself, but also for the joy of it, for the communion of our souls, those rare and beautiful moments. I went back to bed still aching for you, still wearing your shirt because it's as close to you as I can be. And I couldn't help it, I cried myself back to sleep.

Today I feel numb, numb and empty. I fill my mind with little thoughts, keep myself busy with an endless number of small tasks that I am able to complete. I suppose that it helps to assuage the frustration of not being able to change the fact that you are not here with me. There is nothing I can do about it and I rail against my impotence. I cannot grow accustomed to waiting. So I no longer look to an unknown point in the distant future when you may return, but only to this day. If not this day, then maybe the next. And thus, for the most part, I keep my uneasy peace.

Until tomorrow,
Rebecca

Dearest Love, 19 August 1864

    I have received a letter from Rachel Carr Moffatt today, Darling, wife of your cousin Luther in Nashville. It was delivered to Charles' and Alma's by way of a friend of Charles and they gave it to me today when I visited. The mail service here is so poor as to be almost nonexistent, so its' arrival was something of an event in itself! It is the first letter I have received in over a year. I was taken aback to realize how much my scope of awareness has been diminished by the war. I have not thought of Luther and Rachel or anything else outside of my narrow existence for the longest time. The letter was two months old, but quite long and full of news. In it Rachel told a story that I must relate to you, Augustus.

    When the war broke out your cousin swore that he would not bear arms against either side. Though he was born and raised in Massachusetts, he chose to move south and make his home here. Then he married Rachel, a southern girl from a prominent family there in Nashville. He decided to join the Union army, Dear, and volunteered for the federal prison there in Nashville. The army allowed him to do this not only because his paralyzed thumb made it difficult to shoot a gun, but also because of his knowledge of the shoe business. The prisoners make shoes there, right at the prison. They slaughter the cattle, butcher their own meat, tan the hides for leather, and make shoes for the Union army. Luther was made overseer of the shoe shop.

    You know what a good, fair, and generous man Luther is. He is very highly regarded by his men and the prisoners alike for his treatment of them. He befriended one of the prisoners in particular, a Captain Anderson from Atlanta, a farmer before the war, who was captured at the battle of Stones River. Luther made the captain supervisor in the shoe shop to ensure that the men were overseen and worked by one of their own.

The captain was impressed with Luther's concern for the treatment and welfare of the prisoners and his efforts to improve their conditions. Wanting to repay Luther's kindness and knowing that Luther was married to a southern girl, the captain made an anniversary gift with his own hands for Luther and Rachel. It is a bonnet box. It measures eighteen inches wide, twelve inches high, and twelve inches deep. He made it of yellow and black poplar, nailed it together with shoe tacks, and covered it with some of the leather made there at the prison.

Before the captain was able to finish it Luther discovered what he was doing and decided to help him along with it. Luther bought some dark blue velvet to line the box with and a mirror for the inside of the lid. The captain told Luther that he would enjoy decorating the box, as one of his hobbies was whittling and carving. So Luther gave the man his own pocket knife and the captain carved pieces of cow bone into decorations for the box.

It has a saw tooth border on the top and all sides, hearts in the corners, and a sunburst on the top. The front has a diamond within the saw tooth rectangle with a heart in the center. The keyhole is centered in three interlocking ovals, symbol of the Odd Fellows Lodge of which Luther is a member.

Rachel said that Luther was touched beyond words when the captain presented him with the finished box. She was quite moved as well. Luther even asked her to keep it in the front parlor where it can be seen instead of putting it in her dressing room. She agrees that it should be seen and its story should be told. Being something of an artist herself she even drew a picture of it. It is a beautiful thing, Augustus.

Why is it so easy to slaughter nameless, faceless men wearing the wrong color uniform? Because they are anonymous does that negate their humanity? Had Luther and the captain met on the battlefield they would have tried to kill each other. Even in prison they are still enemies. Yet one on one they somehow rose above it and became friends. Give them names and faces, acknowledge their humanity and it changes things, doesn't it?

Both the north and south claim to have God on their side. How it must offend his ear to hear pious, self-righteous hypocrites invoke His name to justify their murderous deeds! It sickens me so to hear it. Anyone who says such things is a fool and has no credibility with me. What has God to do with this war? God didn't start this war and He doesn't fight on either side. This war is of man and Satan himself. It's only in small stories like this one that I can see anything approaching godliness. How many stories are there like this one, Augustus? I've heard enough of them to give some small cause for hope. As I have said before, the human soul can be an amazing thing. Even in the meanest of circumstances that spark of divinity can shine if given a chance. If only we'd learn.

I read the letter aloud to Charles and Alma, not realizing its contents might hurt them. I expected it to anger Charles that his cousin had joined with the Union, but he reacted in a way I didn't expect. He cried. Sad, silent tears. I felt so bad for hurting him and tried to apologize for being so insensitive but he stopped me and hugged me and told me it was not my fault, or even Luther's fault. It was the war. He even apologized to me for losing his composure and tried to joke about acting like an old woman. He is more of his old self these days, Darling, but he is still haunted.

Strangely, Rachel's letter was some comfort to me. The Yankee is still here with us. It's been nine days now; he is healing well from what Belle tells me. Samson and Joseph still keep a close eye on him though he has expressed nothing but gratitude toward us. I sent word to him through Samson that we will take him to the Yankees in town as soon as he is well enough to travel. At least he can speak for himself as to how he incurred his wounds and attest to his treatment here as well if necessary.

Though my mind is more restful having made a decision, it still unnerves me having him here. You say that I am too good hearted, Augustus, but I will admit to being something of a coward. I know well what could happen if the wrong people found that he was here and knew of the aid I had given him. Nor could I expect Mary or Charles and Alma to understand after what they have suffered at the Yankees' hands. So he will leave soon. Samson can take him in at night. Whether I've done right or wrong I'll soon be relieved of the burden. I only know that I had to do as my heart dictated whatever the consequence. I do not pray for victory, I pray only for your return. And yes, Augustus, I do hope that by sending another woman's husband back to her the Lord will notice and see fit to send mine back to me.

Another day passes,
Rebecca

My Love,   24 August 1864

    Finally I am relieved of the guilty secret I have carried for the past two weeks; the Yankee is gone. He sent word to me through Samson that he felt ready to leave, his wounds having healed enough not to break open from the trip in the dogcart. With the aid of a crutch Samson fashioned for him he is even able to walk a short distance. Though I felt it was premature I did not make any effort to stop him. Indeed, I had Samson take him in to town that very night, just last night.

    They waited until ten o'clock before setting out and Samson encountered no one on the trip. The major would not even allow Samson to drive him up in front of headquarters for fear it would be discovered who had rendered him aid. With the help of the crutch and the hitching rails, the major made his way down the street. Samson turned the cart around and told me that the last time he looked back the major had almost reached the sleeping sentry in front of headquarters.

    So he is gone and I am grateful. He was not found, nothing happened. I suppose that my feeling of two weeks ago can be attributed to nothing more than my own distress and guilt for having him here and giving him aid. I only know that I feel weak with relief that it is over. Already it seems like a dream. I only spoke with him once. Perhaps in time I can convince myself that it was only a bad dream, that I did not truly commit such a traitorous act. Perhaps.

Now I can return to the normal routine of our day to day existence, living with our accustomed and familiar fears. Those have been with us for so long now that it is even possible for me to ignore them at times. How strange it is for us to accept as a way of life something we would never imagine we could even endure and stranger still that we would become accustomed to it. But the business of life goes on, Augustus, whatever the circumstance.

The garden is at its peak now and keeps us busy. We dry much more of our produce now as canning jars are so difficult to obtain. We've had a good yield this year, the Yankees notwithstanding. The beans and tomatoes have done well. We were able to salvage more of the field crop than we expected, so we have yams and corn. Thankfully, it appears that we will have enough to take us through the winter. Lately Mary has begun to help us with the garden. She especially enjoys my flowers, and even chides me for "growing" the morning glories! I believe it has helped her find some peace. The work itself is nurturing. It seems to raise her spirits and make her feel more a part of us. She joins in our conversations easily now, even smiling occasionally. She cares for and plays with Shane much more and seems to truly relate to him. I have helped her make him some clothes, and have shown her how to smock. She seems to enjoy it, and stitches beautifully. Slowly she is healing.

Shane is an adorable baby, Darling, extremely good natured. Though he is showered with love and seems happy, it breaks my heart that he will grow up without knowing his father, and that Phillip did not live to see his fine baby boy or watch him grow to manhood. The most tragic thing about this war is the loss the poor children will have to suffer through no fault of their own. Loss of wisdom and guidance, loss of discipline, loss of the love of their fathers. Thousands upon thousands of them, northern and southern. Innocent children will pay the consequence of our folly, know the pain of loss and never know the joy of family. How can victory compensate for such loss, no matter who claims it? Can a victory make up for what their fathers would have given them? Never in their lifetimes, Augustus, it's an irreplaceable loss that will even affect their own children.

Yet another reason you must come home to us, Dear. Though Shane is not your son, he is your nephew and will grow up here with us. He needs a man to teach him, a man he can emulate. How much he could learn about being a man from you! You would teach him that knowledge is a thing worthy of pursuit, that dreams are precious and attainable, that being sensitive to others brings great understanding, that there is great strength in gentleness, and how good humor can add so much joy to life. He would do well to be half the man that you are, my love. I know you will gladly do all that you can for him, as much as if he were your own son. It's your way, and one of the reasons I love you as I do. We both need you back.

Working outside today I could sense the faintest twinge of fall. The air is clear, it gives a different quality to light, making images and colors sharper and brighter. The haze of summer is lifting; the heat of the day does not linger after dark. Almost imperceptibly the days have shortened. If I watch toward the woods I will see the occasional tell-tale leaf let go and float to the ground.

So the endless procession of long, hot days that we see ahead of us every May proves again to be limited after all. The goldenrod is blooming, the corn has tasseled, and the apples have ripened. To be sure, we'll have Indian summer yet, but I feel time growing short, fall will soon be upon us. Spring always makes me feel that I have all the time in the world, and all of the possibilities. Fall tells me that I haven't. It makes me restless, even more than I have been of late. I think of things I yet want to do, the books I want to read, the places I want to see.

And I think of regrets. They are funny things, Augustus. I find that it is not the things I have done that I regret, it is the things I have not done. It is the words I did not speak, the kindness I didn't do, the love I didn't share. All of the opportunities that I let slip by. If I ever get you back, Darling, I will live whatever precious time we have together so that I'll have no more regrets. Then perhaps fall will no longer make me feel restless, but content and happy.

Always,
Rebecca

Augustus, my life,   29 August 1864

    Today, my darling, after almost three years with no word of you I hear that you may have been captured and taken prisoner, and I am frantic with worry! What have they done to you, Augustus? Is it you after all? They tell me they don't even know with certainty. How could they not? I must calm myself. I must think clearly, put down all of the facts, those few I have, and I must do something. I have to find the whole truth somehow.

    A Yankee patrol was here today, a sarcastic and insensitive sergeant and two men. The sergeant rudely questioned me about you, where you were, whom you were with, divisions, brigades, detachments. The last I knew of you, you were with Bedford Forrest. From what news we have heard he has been all over west Tennessee, northern Alabama, Georgia, and Mississippi. I haven't the slightest idea where you are, or even if you are still with him. Troops are reassigned and reorganized all the time, especially considering the thousands of casualties we have suffered. I told the sergeant as much and told him also that I had not had word from you in over two years. With a derisive snort the sergeant addressed one of his men and told him outright that he believed me to be a liar.

    Then turning back to me he said that it was of no matter because it had been reported that you had been captured in fighting near Atlanta. A Captain Moffitt was among the prisoners, badly wounded and unable to speak for himself. One of the men taken with the captain said the wounded man was from west Tennessee, but knew little else of him.

I asked the sergeant if he had a description of the man. Did he have red hair and a red beard, was his first name Augustus, were they sure the name was spelled correctly? Augustus, he laughed at me! He sat on his horse, threw back his head, and roared with laughter! Then he mockingly asked me if I supposed that they drew him a nice little picture of all of the prisoners. I have never met a more contemptuous creature in all of my life. The sergeant then proceeded to explain to me in the most condescending manner that he only had a list of names, and his job was to attempt to locate family members and advise them of the prisoners' whereabouts. All of the prisoners on his list were taken to a prison camp in St. Louis. I told him I would go to St. Louis and see if it was you, and bring you home if you were wounded.

He did not laugh then. He stared at me for a full minute, hatred burning in his eyes. Then he spat on the ground. Leaning toward me from his horse, he raised his voice as if speaking to a deaf person and informed me again that the man was taken to a prison, not a hotel where he could check out whenever he wished. He asked me who the hell I thought I was that I could just sashay through Yankee lines at my will. He leaned back in his saddle then, and grinned in a way that chilled my blood. Speaking to me again, this time in a lower tone, he told me not to worry myself unduly. If it was you after all, you would make you own way home after the war. If you lived that long.

At that moment, Augustus, I could have killed the man with my bare hands and enjoyed every minute of it. I might have tried, had I not thought his companions would have stopped me. As it was, I was trembling. I couldn't even speak. I could feel hot tears stinging my eyes. I walked with faltering steps up to his horse, placed my hand on its shoulder to steady myself, turned my face up to him and whispered "Lieutenant..." The fool was actually flattered, and I'm sure mistook the tears in my eyes for fear. When he leaned over toward me to hear what I might say I spat in his face. He immediately drew back his whip and would surely have struck me, but the man on his right quickly lunged over and restrained him. Without another word he savagely jerked the reins back and wheeled his horse around, knocking me to the ground, and digging his spurs into the animal he galloped off, his men close behind him. I doubt they will return, unless it is for revenge. They even forgot to steal anything while they were here.

I quickly got up and brushed myself off, unhurt from the fall. As I turned to go back into the house Samson and Joseph were coming down the steps, clearly shocked by the altercation. They had witnessed the entire ugly scene. Samson was furious and Joseph had tears in his eyes. We spoke not a word, but went into the parlor where we found Belle and Lizbeth comforting Mary, who was sobbing as if her heart would break again. They too had seen and heard everything from the parlor windows.

I was frightened at the fury I felt inside of me, Augustus. I know now exactly what a blind rage is. It rose, hot and black, monstrous, blocking out everything else. Something had to give; something had to before I did. I walked stiffly to the kitchen using every ounce of strength within me to hold myself together. I picked up the first plate I could reach from our interrupted and forgotten lunch and smashed it to the floor. I followed it with another, and then a glass before Belle stopped me, wrapping her arms around me, hugging me hard and close. After a few minutes the fury abated, burned itself out. Through bitter tears I remember telling her that I was sorry that I could not think of anything cruder and more base to do to that man than spitting in his face. She told me that from where she was it looked like I did just fine. It was enough to run three Yankees off, wasn't it?

That finally broke the tension and we went back to the parlor. Poor Mary was calmer but still crying. I sat next to her and held her for a few minutes before Lizbeth gently coaxed her into going upstairs to lie down for a little while. It was only then that the true magnitude of the Yankee's news finally registered fully in my consciousness. You may be wounded, Augustus, so badly that you cannot even speak for yourself. You made it to the prison camp, but that has been some two weeks ago. You might have died since then. And yet, it may not even be you in the prison camp at all, but some other Captain Moffitt. The name is spelled differently than ours. If you were still with Forrest, why did the men captured with you not know you? The sergeant provided me with no detail. No answers.

Is it you, Augustus, is it really you? And what am I to do? How could they be so callous as to come out here and tell me such a thing without knowing for certain it was true? Was it a deliberate act of hatred and spite designed to make me suffer so? We have heard stories of the prison camps, Augustus, and their appalling conditions. Men swear that their chances are better on a battlefield. I am sick with fear of what may happen to you there.

Samson, Joseph, Belle, and I have gone over the news again and again. We discussed all kinds of possibilities, talking late into the night. For now we have decided the only action we can take is to go to the telegraph office in Union City and try to send a telegram to St. Louis. If I provide them a description it may be possible for them to ascertain whether it is truly you and put my anguish to rest. Samson will drive me tomorrow. It seems such a poor effort, and I have little faith that it will affect any action on the Yankees' part. But I must do something. I cannot come to you, and I cannot sit idly by and wait for the war to end. If you are wounded, Darling, you need me now. If it is not you, then I have to know that, too.

We will leave early in the morning for Union City. I must get there as quickly as I am able. The day after I will have Samson take me to see Charles and Alma. I must tell them what news I have. I am in hopes that Charles may be able to offer some insight into my dilemma and perhaps help me decide a course of action. You are his own dear brother and he would give his life for you without a second thought. As would I, my love. Together we will think of something. Somehow we will find the truth, find you. If it is you in the prison camp, Augustus, I beg you to fight for your life, hold tight to it until I can find a way to help you. And I promise you, Darling, I will.

My strength and love are yours,
Rebecca

My Dearest, 31 August 1864

I am exhausted, my darling, near collapse. I have slept not a wink these past two nights. For two days I have tried everything I could think of to no avail. I am met with ridicule, derision, and failure at every turn. Samson drove me to Union City yesterday, where there is a telegraph office at the post office. The Yankees have taken it as their headquarters now, for use of the telegraph.

When I arrived the sentry, a private, would not even let me inside to speak to the officer in charge. Nor would he call for an officer of higher rank to come out and speak with me. He told me that the telegraph is only to be used for official Union business. I tried to explain to him that it is official Union business as the Yankees may have my husband in a Union prison camp in St. Louis, and I must find out for sure. He curtly informed me that determining the whereabouts of Rebel prisoners was not official business.

I could feel my frustration rising, but kept my composure, trying to reason with the sentry. I explained that the information came to me from a Union dispatch in the first place, intending to officially inform me about my husband. He countered that if that were the case they would send more information when they had it, these things would be handled in their proper priority. Then he told me I should just be a good wife and go home and wait further word. I knew he was not about to lift a finger to help me.

Glancing back toward the building I noticed another man standing at the window. I could make out his form behind the curtain. I supposed he was the officer in charge, satisfying his curiosity. Hoping this to be the case I called out to him, begging him to come outside and speak with me. He walked away from the window and never came out.

Once more I tried to entreat the sentry to help me, but now he would not even turn his face to me. At this point my frustration overcame my composure. Turning back to the building I called out again to the officer inside and told him what cowards I thought the Union had for officers if they couldn't even face one lone southern woman, and how spiteful they were not to help even though it required so little effort on their part. I accused them of being neglectful of their duties not to follow up on their own dispatch. I couldn't even provoke him into coming outside and I only succeeded in further enraging the sentry.

By now there were several people standing about in the street, wordlessly watching the scenario. Without speaking to me the sentry told Samson through clenched teeth that if he did not take me away at once he would lock me up himself for trying to incite public unrest. From his tone of voice I knew he meant it. There was nothing else I could do. Having utterly failed, we left and returned home.

Today Samson drove me to Charles and Alma's. They saw at once my distress and were themselves alarmed. I told them the whole grim story, all about the sergeant who came to the house, the news of you, and of my trip to Union City. Charles was visibly shaken; he knew the dire nature of your plight. As much as it hurt him to admit it, he told me the Yankee was right. They would never let me through their lines, and they would not release you. While enlisted men were sometimes released and allowed to go home, officers were not. He agreed that my only hope was that they might have sent the telegram. He weakly suggested that I might write a letter, but we both knew the futility of his suggestion. We could think of no other way that I might find the truth before it might be too late for you. Though none of us spoke these last words aloud they were foremost in our minds.

Then Charles brightened and with a shrug of his shoulders said that we may be worrying needlessly. He talked about how strong you are, and how resourceful you are, assuring me that you have always been well able to take care of yourself. It was as much for himself as for me that he talked on in this manner, trying to give us both some kind of hope. It was as if he did not hear me tell of how badly you may be wounded.

Though it hurt me to see him do this, it also angered me. I will not be pacified like a child. I do not want to hear comforting lies. We will discuss it no more. If Charles is not able to face the truth, so be it, I can understand. But I must face it, and I will brook no compromise or defeat where it concerns you, Augustus.

There has to be something I can do, it only remains for me to find it. Alma sensed my feeling and its import; we spoke in the kitchen while preparing dinner. She even tried to apologize for Charles. I do not blame Charles and told her so, no apology was necessary. I made it clear to her, however, that I would do whatever I might think of to find you, to find the truth. She understands.

At dinner Charles shared some gossip around town concerning a Yankee officer, a major, who had been missing and then turned up at Yankee headquarters in the middle of the night. He had been shot and had obviously received aid somewhere as his wounds were tended and half healed. Yet he refused to say where he had been while he was missing. The major left town two days ago, headed north this time. He even knew the officer's name and repeated it.

It was not until I heard the name spoken aloud did I realize he was speaking of the Yankee in the barn. With so much on my mind I was paying scant attention to the conversation. So great was my shock that I dropped my fork on my plate. I had forgotten the Yankee! Only nine days gone and it already seems a lifetime ago. I excused myself for being weary and overwrought and Charles quickly apologized for being insensitive and oafish and then turned the conversation to their little garden. The children happily joined in with their plans for next year. I was grateful for their chatter; it gave me time to collect myself. I was surprised that they did not read the guilt on my face and understand its meaning. But the talk was nothing more than idle gossip. They did not know the truth and I knew that they would soon be bored with it. Nevertheless, after dinner when they pressed me to stay the night I hastily declined, explaining that I could not leave Mary alone. It relieved me immensely to leave them.

Samson and I rode a good way in silence, then he opened up to me. It shames me to admit that I had not realized how discomposed he is over the news of you. I have been too distraught to notice. He feels almost as frustrated and helpless as I. He, too, would do anything he could for you. Augustus, he even offered to go to St. Louis to get you. While it is true that the Yankees would likely allow him to pass through their lines, there is still nothing he could do to accomplish your release. Even so, I was touched by his offer and told him as much. I know that you would be as well.

We fell silent again, each to our own thoughts of you. As daylight faded to darkness it felt like fading hope. Though it fades I will not let it slip my grasp. I cannot. At last the strain of the last two days finally caught up with me. I fell asleep sitting up, leaning on Samson's shoulder.

Your,
Rebecca

My love, my life,   7 September 1864

    Seven anguishing days have passed, Darling, since I last wrote. I have had no answers, no relief, no peace. But today my intuition of four weeks ago, my feeling that something was happening of which I was not then fully aware, is finally borne out. It was not of my control but I now know the part I will play; I know what I must do and how I must go about it. I will set it all out just as it happened so you will know the whole course of events.

    Yesterday morning we were working in the garden when I heard the sound of horses coming up the drive. Judging it to be at least three horses, maybe four, I knew it could only be the Yankees. I glanced over toward Mary and Lizbeth. Mary was kneeling not far from me and seemed frozen in movement, her hands held out in front of her. Lizbeth slowly straightened from the tomato plants and looked over at me. They were thinking the same as I. Telling them to hurry and take the vegetables into the house, I rose and brushed my hands off on my apron, then walked around the house, stopping in front of the porch just as the four men reined their horses in. One of the men dismounted, ordering the others to remain mounted and stand ground. He then quickly strode straight toward me. My heart was already in my throat. I had been expecting the sergeant to take his revenge in some manner and was awaiting it.

    The man had covered half the distance to me when I recognized him. Again I thought of you. The red beard – Major Gardner! I was too stunned to react so thankfully did not give myself away. He tipped his hat to me and addressed me formally, then nodded for me to walk with him to the side of the house, out of earshot of his men.

The major was still at headquarters in Troy the day the sergeant came to the house, and heard that horrible man's account of the incident afterwards. Apparently the man was indeed intent on extracting his measure of vengeance with a real southern bonfire, as he called it, and bragged loudly about it. The major informed him that he would do no such thing. Union sentiment has always been present, even if not prominent, in this area; hence many here have remained relatively unmolested compared to the Deep South. The Union was in control here now and there was little trouble, therefore the sergeant was to do nothing that might alienate that sentiment. Furthermore, the major warned him that if any harm came to me or mine that he would hold the sergeant personally responsible, court martial him, and throw him in lockup. Evidentially the sergeant took him at his word.

Knowing now that you may have been wounded and captured the major went the next day to Union City headquarters and did indeed send a telegram to St. Louis in an attempt to ascertain whether it was truly you. The prison is under the charge of a Major Ayers, a friend of Major Gardner's and fellow classmate from West Point. During his stay here it seems the major learned a great deal about us from Belle and Samson. He knew that he resembled you closely; he knew the similarities and the differences and therefore could give a detailed description of you, down to the old scar on the underside of your left forearm. To impress upon his friend the urgency of his inquiry he told him how I had saved his life and explained that he meant to repay his debt in kind.

Then he waited for a reply. He was there in Union City when I arrived, only a day after him. It was his form I saw behind the curtain. Fearing that revealing himself to me at that point would have exposed his plan and put it at risk, not to mention putting my safety at risk, he kept silent and waited. Six days it took for him to find the answer. He received it only this morning and came straightaway to the farm.

It is you, Augustus. Now I know. You are gravely wounded but still alive. As he told me all of this he took some papers out of his coat. They were passes, Darling, letters allowing me to pass through Yankee lines and giving me permission to take you out of prison and bring you home. The major drew them up himself while awaiting the reply in the event that they might be needed. All of this he did on his own, involving only Major Ayers in St. Louis. Had his plan been revealed prematurely it could have been misconstrued as treason, he said, much as my own actions could have been. However, he assured me that once written, orders take on a weight of their own, and I needn't fear that they would not be followed.

I asked him only one question, Augustus, how he knew I would go to you. He looked down and was silent for a moment. When he looked back up at me his face had softened somewhat, his expression almost wistful. He surprised me by answering that it was because he knew me.

By the way he was treated when he was here, by what was said and what was not in our single conversation, by the tenacity I displayed in Union City. He had no doubt that if I could treat my enemies as I did, then I would go to the ends of the earth for someone I loved. The major is a very perceptive man. He told me then that he had wired Major Ayers back that I would leave shortly, and to expect me. He smiled then, a smile so much like yours, albeit a sad smile; wished me the best of luck, turned and strode quickly to his horse and mounted. Again he tipped his hat to me, ordered his men about, and then was gone.

Holding the papers tight to my breast I walked back around to the front porch where Samson, Joseph, and Belle waited. They had seen everything but heard nothing. After convincing Mary that the Yankees would do no harm, Lizbeth had taken her to the kitchen to prepare the morning's vegetables and to start lunch. I quickly related to them the whole story. They were as stunned as I at the whole turn of events. I told them that we would tell Mary that they were here only to verify that it was indeed you in the prison camp and to give me the papers to go get you; that I was being allowed to go for you only because you were gravely wounded and could not come home on your own. We need not explain further.

The discussion immediately turned to the trip. Mary and Lizbeth joined us at this point. Of course we are all anxious to do all we can and we all want to make the trip for you. After much discussion we finally decided that Joseph, Belle, and I will make the trip. Mary, Samson, and Lizbeth will remain here. Poor Samson was visibly disappointed, but realizes that he can do much more staying here. The work would be too much for Joseph alone. Mary has little Shane to tend. Her and Lizbeth have become close and do well together. Mary rose to the occasion, bless her. I think the responsibility is exactly what she needs. It gives her purpose and she knows we are depending on her.

We started right away preparing for the trip. We will take Rusty and the dogcart. To spare poor Rusty as much as possible, we decided that two of us will walk and one will ride, taking turns. We will follow the river on the east side and cross at St. Louis. The trip is approximately two hundred fifty miles. Figuring conservatively at fifteen miles a day, it should take us just over two weeks to make the trip, so we will supply for a generous month's provisions. I am thankful now that we have dried so much of our food. We worked feverishly until late and then we all slept restlessly. We awoke early this morning to finish our preparations, for we shall leave tomorrow.

There remained one thing for me to do before I left. I had to go see Charles and Alma and tell them. In doing so I was resolved that my sins would be revealed and I would pay for them at last. Charles knew of the gossip and knew the officer's name. He would insist on seeing the papers and would then know the truth. For what other reason would this very officer write me passes to get my husband out of prison camp? With all of this in mind, a heavy heart and a knot in my stomach, I went to face them. I rode Rusty barebacked and went alone.

When I arrived I stood in their parlor and spoke without flourish. I told them that it had been officially verified that you were in prison and wounded terribly. I told them I had passes to go and get you, and I would leave tomorrow. Charles was incredulous and asked immediately to see the papers, as I knew he would. I handed them over and he read them carefully. When he finished he looked up at me for what seemed the longest time. I met his gaze and did not look away. I offered neither excuse nor explanation. There was so much in his face; disbelief, anger, sadness. Pain. He knew. Slowly he passed the papers to Alma, his eyes never leaving mine. I expected him to strike me, or curse me, but hoarsely he spoke only three words. "They're in order." Then he turned and walked a few steps away. He turned back to me and opened his mouth to speak, but said nothing. He closed his mouth and, dropping his head he turned again and left the room, going upstairs.

By then Alma had finished reading the papers and she knew, too. I could hardly bear it. Before she could say anything I told her that I would offer no apologies or excuses for what I had done, but that responsibility was mine alone. I explained that Mary knew nothing of the Yankee to this very day and took no part in rendering him aid. Without giving her time to respond I continued, telling her that I hoped her and Charles would not make you and Mary suffer for my actions. There had been too much suffering already; we needed each other too much now to split apart as a family. If I was to be condemned I would accept it, but you and Mary are innocent. I told her that I felt there must be something very wrong with the world when acts of mercy are considered traitorous, war or no. I asked her then if she could find it in her heart to look in on Mary occasionally to see that she was all right.

With tears in her eyes and mine by then, she nodded her assent. Quietly she said she would try to talk to Charles. Then she wished me good luck and Godspeed. Unlike Charles, I was unable to read her face; she looked at me as if she had never seen me before. There was no more to be said; I left immediately.

By the time I arrived home all was in readiness for our trip. Samson fed and watered Rusty and put her in the barn. We will have an early supper and retire. All of us are probably too apprehensive to sleep, but we must try to rest. We have a long and difficult journey ahead of us.

So tomorrow, Darling, I will be on my way to you at long last. The very thing I've wanted for so long now yet it hardly seems real. You are alive and I will bring you back. We will find each other again. And we will begin again from there.

Tomorrow brings me closer to you,
Rebecca

My Dearest, 10 September 1864

It is the evening of the third day of our trip. We have made better passage than I hoped thus far; I judge over fifty miles. I am so thankful, Augustus, for I am driven, possessed of an overwhelming need to reach you, to see you and touch you again, to look into your eyes. My need is made all the more intense by the suffocating fear that I may be too late, that I may not reach you in time. I feel that I am racing death, and that if only I can get to you first then I may have you back. My ghosts follow me even here, taunting me every moment that I am not putting one foot in front of the other, making my way to you. I want to push on without stopping but I know that we must rest. Belle and Joseph tire of walking, and we must spare poor Rusty if she is to last the trip. I know I must rest also, but sleep does not come easily.

We have quickly settled into a routine without even having discussed it. As on the first day we start at daybreak after a cold breakfast of cornbread and dried apples. We stop for lunch in a shady spot by the road at the hottest part of the day, unhitching Rusty to graze and rest a little. Boiled meat from our last smoked ham with some vegetables suffices for our lunch. After a half-hour's rest we start again, traveling until about an hour before sunset, when we start watching for a place to stop for the night. We're careful to pick a spot where our fire will not be seen from the road, or from any house that may be nearby. Joseph tends to feeding and watering Rusty while Belle and I prepare supper. I tease her about how well she can cook over a campfire, even making our cornbread without an oven. She teases me about how well I sleep on the ground. But she watches me closely; she knows that I do not sleep well.

We talk for a little while after supper, quietly, intimately. Joseph is his usual reticent self, most often just nodding, but occasionally adding his thoughts to our conversation. I'm so glad they are with me, Augustus. They are so strong, in such different ways. Belle doesn't hesitate to speak her mind, sometimes sharply but always with wisdom and love. She keeps me calm and rational. Joseph in his quiet way works right along and always gets the job done. He's so sure and dependable, and I find that comforting. I know the trip is difficult for both of them, yet there was never the first question but that they would walk every step of the way with me.

Watching them tonight I've noticed they have aged and I wonder when it happened. Are they really getting old or has the war made them look older? I'm not sure. I may have to come right out and ask Belle how old they are, if I ever work up enough courage. I'm sure you might imagine how she would answer if I put such a question to her!

Tonight we spoke of Mary. It worries me leaving her there but I have no other choice. Belle is confident that she will be fine. She spoke aloud to my silent fear that she may have to face a Yankee patrol. With Lizbeth and Samson there Belle feels that she will bear up to it. She reminded me of Mary's stubborn streak, and believes it will serve her well if needed. She reminded me, too, that Mary had made her way to us from Memphis alone with a small baby and through lots of Yankees.

I thought of the morning we left. Though she shed a few tears, Mary had that determined set to her chin that she always affected once she had put her mind to something. She told me to hurry to you. They would be fine, she said, she would finish out the garden for me and even take care of the flower seeds for next year. With a smile she told me I needn't worry about them, for she and Lizbeth had Samson and her little man to take care of them. And then she gave me a brave little smile. She is so dear to me, Augustus, and has been through so much already. I couldn't bear anything else happening to her. Talking to Belle did make me feel easier about it, though. Again, in her way, Belle calmed me. I had to smile then, too.

Thus far our trip has been uneventful. The weather has been quite clement. The ease of our trip so far seems only to add to my apprehension. Belle warns me not to go buying trouble, there's plenty around for free, and says it will be of no help to you if I drive us all mad on this journey. She's right, of course, but I can hardly help myself. Under different circumstance I would even consider this something of an adventure. But instead of being open to and inquisitive about the surroundings, the people we encounter, and the new experience I find that I am closed to it all. I only notice what is around me in terms of how it may harm us or slow our progress. I am of single mind and purpose, and that is all that matters to me. Nothing else is important to me now, and nothing will distract me from what I have set out to do. Only when I have you back and know that you are safe will the rest of my life have any import.

We camped the first night near the north end of Reelfoot Lake, on the west side. We could see the Yankee fortification on the river; it seemed there was little activity. No one disturbed us. The second night we were in Kentucky, a little south of Hickman. Again we were undisturbed. We passed around the outskirts of town and continued north yesterday without being stopped or questioned by what few people we encountered, all civilians. They seemed to regard us with either suspicion or mild curiosity, but not enough of either to as much as speak to us. I am glad of that. I know the Union sentiment is much stronger here, and I would trust no one. To this point the only Yankees we have seen are those troops traveling on the river, north and south. They are considerable in number.

Today we passed through Columbus, where we saw many Yankees, I suppose because of the rail line from the Mississippi to Nashville. I expected every one of them to challenge us and perhaps even turn us about and send us home, but we passed through town without being challenged even once. We were a couple of miles out of town when I wondered aloud that we had walked right by so many Yankees and had not been stopped. Belle huffily remarked that those Yankees weren't all so smart if they couldn't even recognize us for the threat that we could be! I looked at her as if she had lost her reason. Us a threat to the Yankees? The thought struck me suddenly as absolutely hysterical. I began to giggle, then to laugh. Belle started to laugh and that just made me laugh harder, until the tears were running down my cheeks. Even Joseph chuckled over it. We had to stop for a few minutes until we could regain our composure before continuing, a little lighter of heart, our nerves a little less taut.

We saw plentiful evidence of the war at the beginning of the trip, many burned and abandoned houses and buildings. Most of the farms were in a general state of neglect. As we traveled north the conditions improved somewhat, though we still see a number of abandoned homes and farms. They seem sad and forgotten. And what of all the people uprooted and displaced by the war? I imagine that many of them, both northern and southern, lived good lives and never harmed anyone, only to have this scourge descend on them and drive them out of their very homes with no say at all in the matter. That is assuming they were fortunate enough to walk away. I feel a dread certainty that many innocent people have paid with their lives for this war in which they had no part. War is always hardest on the innocent.

Tonight we are camped just a few miles south of Fort Jefferson. I am most apprehensive for I feel that tomorrow we will have to face what we have avoided to this point, a Yankee interrogation. My papers are in order and sufficient, what I fear is that some Yankee may yet cause trouble simply because it is in his power to do so. I haven't forgotten the sergeant. I keep my papers with me, tucked inside my bodice where they are safe. They are my passage to you and I guard them with my life. For you are my life, Augustus, my breath, my blood, my reason. I make my way to you to find myself, to find us, that we may truly live again. Hold on to your life, Darling, my life. Hold tightly to me.

My love,
Rebecca

Augustus, my love, 14 September 1864

It has only been four days since I last wrote yet it seems longer, so much has happened. As I anticipated, we were indeed stopped and challenged the morning after my last letter, as we approached Fort Jefferson. There were a number of mounted soldiers on the roadway near the gates to the fort, stopping passersby and checking them.

I saw a group of four soldiers stop a man walking with a young boy perhaps ten or twelve years old. After some discussion one of the soldiers suddenly kicked the man, striking him down in the road. He then ordered the man to his feet and the soldiers took him into the fort, leaving the poor boy standing alone in the road. I cannot imagine what transpired between them, but found it frightening.

My attention was diverted then as we ourselves were approached by two soldiers on horseback. One of them was a sergeant (Lord, please deliver me from any more sergeants in the future!) who demanded that we show our identification and explain our business here. I showed him my papers and Joseph and Belle showed him theirs as well.

He spoke first to them, and talked to them as if they were children, Augustus, asking them if they knew they were free and what that meant. I was surprised that Belle did not give him an earful, but she was quiet. Joseph stepped up to the sergeant and, without removing his hat, asked him if that meant that they were free to go anywhere they wished and do anything they wanted, if it was within the law, of course. The sergeant replied that it did, and Joseph answered in the most serious manner that he reckoned he was free all right, because he was standing in the very spot that he most wanted to be. Belle had to cough to hide her chuckle, and I dared not look at her. The sergeant's face reddened and he stuttered a little, unsure of whether or not he was being had.

He then turned his attention to me. Needlessly raising his voice, he spoke sharply and quite rudely. Confused as to why I would have passes from a Yankee officer to have a Confederate officer released from prison, he seemed most vexed with me. He did not appear inclined to simply allow us to walk away, but didn't seem to know exactly what to do about it, either. Perhaps he was weighing the consequence to his career of crossing the major who had signed the orders.

I believe that my impatience to get to you had finally overcome my fear of the Yankees. Though I thought better of spitting in his face, I did not want to give him the opportunity to make an unfavorable decision, so I spoke up almost as loudly as he and told him that I wanted to see his commanding officer. Apparently he had not yet considered this answer to his dilemma, for he seemed relieved that I had suggested it. Gruffly he ordered us to follow him, and then led us right into the fort. Following him, I glanced back curiously to where the young boy had stood. He was gone.

I don't know whether it was a large fort, but it certainly seemed so to me, and was quite intimidating. There were hundreds of soldiers, and as many horses, some drilling on a large parade ground directly in front of us, others moving purposefully about. It felt as if most of them were staring at us. To the right of the parade grounds were row upon row of tents; barracks, I assumed. To the left and facing the parade ground was a row of buildings that must have served as offices and perhaps officers' quarters. The sergeant led us to one of these small buildings and told us to wait outside. He went inside for a few minutes and then opened the door and called me inside. When Joseph and Belle moved to come in with me he stopped them and told them to wait outside. With confidence I did not feel, I assured them I would be all right, and I went in alone.

I entered the room and the sergeant pointed to a lieutenant seated at a desk directly in front of me. Behind him and to my right was a door to another room. The door was standing slightly ajar, but I could not see into the room itself. Curtly and belligerently the lieutenant stated that the papers seemed quite irregular and asked how I came to have the passes. Briefly I told him the story and added that I would very much appreciate his allowing us to leave without further delay as we still had a long way to go and time was critical. Before the lieutenant could answer me I heard a voice tell him to do as I asked and to get about it quickly.

Startled, I looked toward the door, which was now standing open, and saw another officer standing there. He walked over to the desk and introduced himself as Colonel Rice. Politely he apologized for the inconvenience, and assured me that I would be delayed no longer. The lieutenant had yet to move, he just sat there staring at the colonel with his mouth hanging open. Suddenly the colonel turned to him and thundered "What's the matter, lieutenant? I think one Confederate captain for a Union major is a pretty good trade, don't you?" Augustus, I fairly jumped out of my skin! The lieutenant jerked like he'd been shot, snapped his mouth shut, grabbed my papers and thrust them at me. But instead of taking them, I found my voice, and with all of the fortitude I could muster I told the colonel I wanted him to sign that he had passed me through the fort. Surprised, he inquired why, and I explained that the more Yankee signatures I had on the orders the less trouble I felt I would encounter, and I had no intention of being delayed by every Yankee between Fort Jefferson and St. Louis. Without another word he took the papers and signed them, then handed them to the lieutenant to sign as well! I thanked him, took my papers and left. As I shut the door I glanced back to see the lieutenant still staring after me and the colonel walking back to his office, shaking his head.

Joseph, Belle, and I left quickly without further hindrance. Once outside the fort I explained what had taken place. Belle was jubilant, she thought the idea of the signatures was truly inspired, and told me she couldn't have done better herself. Joseph was shaking his head, too. Seeing it twice now made me wonder what the gesture meant, but I didn't dare ask. I don't think I want to know. I looked back once, wondering fleetingly about the young boy, but there was no sign of him.

It was midafternoon when we approached Fort Holt, situated at the junction of the Ohio and Mississippi rivers. We would have to cross here to Cairo and continue northward from there. It seemed there were fewer soldiers milling about here, and none seemed to be questioning what few civilians we saw. Even so, as we came closer to the fort I noticed a soldier sitting astride a horse just outside the gate. He appeared to be watching us, and I braced myself for another interrogation as he walked his horse over to us. He tipped his hat with a smile and asked if I was Rebecca Moffatt. When I replied that I was, he informed us that he was assigned to escort us to the river and see us across. Colonel Rice had wired from Fort Jefferson and requested the escort!

The soldier was a very young lieutenant and he did his job with great enthusiasm. He had the air of a youngster who has an unexpected holiday from school and chores. Leading us to the docks he informed us that the colonel felt that we might have some difficulty crossing the river as the ferries charged exorbitant fees just now for passage. Moreover, soldiers had priority if there were no military boats available and there were always soldiers needing to cross. We would be crossing in a military boat as there was one preparing to leave shortly. Military boat indeed! It was a confiscated steamboat. Not that I was about to complain, I hadn't anticipated any trouble crossing and was glad for the assistance. I figured the Yankees owed us at least as much.

The boy was friendly and talkative, telling us much about himself. He is from Boston, and only this year came of age to go into proper service, receiving his commission by virtue of his good grades and his father's money. Fort Holt was his first experience with the war; he had seen no action yet but was sure he was up to it and was eagerly anticipating his first real battle. I've no idea how the colonel phrased his wire, but it was obvious the boy did not realize we were Confederates. There are, after all, a considerable number of Union soldiers with southern accents. Perhaps he thought we were relations of the colonel's. We saw no reason to explain ourselves to him.

He is so young, Darling, so naïve, thinking he is a part of something glorious. I doubt he has ever imagined anything close to the horrors he will likely see before it is over. He should be back in Boston where his biggest worries would be his grades and which pretty girl to woo. I don't think he even shaves.

Once at the docks he efficiently saw Rusty and the cart loaded and the showed us to the passenger deck. It seemed strange to be traveling with all those Yankee soldiers, but I am quickly getting over my fear; I won't let it unsettle me. As we are now well into enemy territory I am resolved that I must get accustomed to it. I thought of Mary and Charles and felt a pang of guilt. Then I thought of you and realized that nothing, no amount of fear or guilt, will deter me from finding you. We crossed quietly and no one disturbed us, though we garnered some curious glances. I thank goodness that those Yankees are by no means gentlemen. No one could accuse them of being mannerly.

Disembarking at Cairo I was amazed at the city. I imagine that it is as large as Memphis, and it seemed an industrious and busy place. It looked to me as if half the Union army was there. The lieutenant told us that one of the army's largest training camps was located just outside of

Cairo. He recovered his horse, Rusty and the cart, and told us to follow him. By this time it was quickly becoming dark. All day the skies had become more and more threatening and it finally began to rain a light drizzle. Joseph got out our oilcloth coats, but the lieutenant had none with him though he seemed oblivious to the rain.

We traveled north and west through the city, along the river again, until we came to the outskirts of town. There we came to what looked like another small city made up of rows of barracks. Our lieutenant told us that it was the soldiers' quarters for the training camp. He led us to the officers section where there were long buildings divided into rooms and showed us a room where we could stay the night. It was small and square, holding four cots and a washbasin. Then he offered to take Rusty to the livery, which was located at the end of our row, telling us that we could claim her when we were ready to leave in the morning. Before leaving he addressed me once more, asking if I had some papers for him to sign. I couldn't help a smile. I gave him the papers, he signed them, and I thanked him for his assistance. He told me that the colonel advised I was on my own from here, but he doubted I would encounter any further difficulty that I would not be able to handle. Again I had to smile. Then he was on his way, whistling as he and Rusty disappeared into the darkness and rain.

That little room seemed quite a luxury to us. While Joseph cleaned up at the pump outside, Belle and I used the washbasin, calling to Joseph twice for fresh water. I felt as if I were carrying half the dirt from Troy to Cairo on my person! Finally cleaned, I felt much better but suddenly realized how exhausted I was. I felt bad for Joseph and Belle, for they must have been exhausted as well, though they said nothing. Belle had taken some food off the cart for our supper and we ate it cold, sitting on the edge of our cots. I could hardly chew I was so tired. As soon as we finished supper we unrolled the bedrolls on the cots and retired. I'm sure I was asleep before my head touched the cot, and remember waking only once during the night, briefly, and noting that it had begun to rain in earnest.

In the morning I awoke about an hour after daybreak to find that Joseph had already gone to collect Rusty and the cart. Belle was up and ready to leave. She said she didn't have the heart to wake me if I could sleep through revelry and half the Union army turning out for mess and training! I was shocked and quite abashed; I never heard a thing! Hastily I ate the breakfast Belle had waiting for me and prepared to leave.

Joseph was waiting with Rusty when we came outside, and grinned as he wished me a hearty good morning. I know my face reddened as I could feel it, but I had to smile back, I knew it was his way of teasing me. It had stopped raining though it looked as if it could start again at any moment. Leaving camp we turned north, traveling once again alongside the river. The road was wet and a little slower but not too difficult.

From Cairo the river runs northwest for about seven miles when it abruptly turns south for a few miles before turning back north, then east, forming something of a peninsula. We reached this point shortly after lunch and decided to leave the river and cross the neck of the peninsula, saving ourselves perhaps two days travel. Taking a wagon road north, we followed it for about six miles before turning northwest to meet the river again just south of Hamburg Landing, expecting it to take us a day to travel. However, shortly after leaving the road it started once more to rain. It was still a light rain, but having perhaps only another hour to travel we decided to start looking for a place to stop for the night.

We picked an oak grove that seemed suitable shelter. Joseph fashioned a tent from the two oilcloth sheets and rope while Belle and I collected the driest wood we could find, stacking it under the wagon, out of the rain. We spread our oilcloth coats over the back of the cart to keep the food dry and put on our wool coats, as it was chill and damp. Belle cooked a large pot of ham and vegetable stew and cornbread for supper. It was hot and delicious, and helped to fight the effects of the poor weather. By then it was raining harder and seemed to have set in for the night. Though not a downpour, it was a steady, soaking rain. We kept a good fire going most of the night for the heat of it, one or another of us adding wood to the fire whenever we awakened.

When we arose yesterday it was still raining steadily, and we knew that it would be impossible to travel. Even if the rain stopped it would be too muddy to make any distance and would only tire us needlessly. But the rain did not cease all day. It made me anxious, Darling, I was chaffing for us to be on our way again. I would pace back and forth under the tent for a while, only a few steps each way, then sit, only to rise and pace again after a few moments. I'm afraid that I wore on Belle's nerves, for after lunch she suggested that I take a nap and rest as much as possible. I lay down only to appease her and promptly fell asleep and slept most of the afternoon. She woke me for dinner and as we ate the rain finally stopped. We retired, hopeful that it was over.

We awoke this morning to find the clouds breaking up and the sun shining through. It certainly helped to dry things up, and we welcomed its warmth. Though we are not able to travel today I could at least walk about away from the tent and thus spare Bell's nerves. I've taken a cough from the dampness and I breathe more easily if I move about.

I cannot help thinking that the two days lost would have put me halfway to you. I still try to content myself with thinking only of this day and try not to think of you in prison, for if I dwell on it I would surely drive us all to death on this trip. All that can be done I am doing, and I must have faith that it has purpose, and that purpose is to bring you home safely. Nevertheless, my ghosts are with me still, and assail my reason constantly. Yet beneath it all I remain hopeful, and I cling to that hope fiercely. For to give it up would be to give you up, Augustus. So I will endure whatever befalls me and I will see you again soon, my love. I will have you back.

Until then,
Rebecca

Dearest Augustus, 　　　　　　　　　19 September 1864

Another five days passing finds me more than halfway to you now. But I am beginning to imagine that the world has lost all of its reason and sanity and has set itself against me. I feel as if I am being punished and I don't know why. While I have been in fear that I might not reach you in time, it has never once occurred to me that I might not reach you at all. I knew the trip could be dangerous, but that danger was vague and undefined. I assumed it would wear a blue uniform. Finally I am in fear of my very life and I find that the danger is very real, and it has a face. It lives and breathes. I can hardly bear to write of what has happened, I wish I could blot it all from my mind. Augustus, I doubt I could live long enough to forget it.

The day after I last wrote we crossed the peninsula and met the river again several miles south of Hamburg Landing. It was still muddy and travel was slow, but it was a worthwhile day. The landscape here is much different than home. West Tennessee is so flat and smooth, with only slight rises and falls in the land. Here the land is very hilly and rough. It is difficult to see a great distance in most places. Perhaps because I am not used to it that it makes me feel closed in, and that makes me feel apprehensive. Or it could be circumstance; we don't know who or what may be around the next hill.

We camped that night in the lee of a hill where there stood a grove of trees. A clearing opened toward the center of the grove, almost closing again before the land dipped toward the river. Joseph unhitched Rusty and took her down to the river for water as Belle and I started supper. It was growing dusk as we ate. Just as we were finishing our meal we heard movement through the trees. We glanced at each other with apprehension in our eyes, and all we could do was wait.

Moments later two men stepped out of the trees and into the clearing, perhaps twenty yards from us. They were both older men and neither wore a uniform. Both, however, were armed, one with a shotgun and the other with a rifle, which they held leveled at us. Joseph, seated on my left near the cart, rose and waited, whispering to Belle and me to remain seated and stay calm. The men approached to within a few feet of the campsite, looking about, I presume, to see if we were armed as well.

I bid them good evening and the man with the rifle told me to hold my tongue, he would tell me whether it was a good evening. He moved closer until he stood in front of me, across the campfire. Looking at the man with the shotgun, he jerked his head toward the cart. The man with the shotgun walked over to the cart and started rummaging through our possessions, the asked us if we had any guns. I replied that we were unarmed, yet he continued his search. When he was finally satisfied that we had no guns he gave up his search and leaned against the cart, keeping his shotgun pointed at Joseph.

The man with the rifle finally turned back to me and demanded to know who we were and what we were doing on his land. I quickly related the story of our trip to St. Louis and finished by telling him that I would appreciate his allowing us to camp for the night, and promised that we would be gone by daybreak. Angrily he replied that he had seen us pass his place and knowing that we were up to no good had followed us. When he saw us leave the road he went back and got his brother for assistance in the event that we wished to cause trouble. I assured him that we meant no harm, wanting only to eat and rest, and apologized again for camping on his land without his expressed permission. As we had crossed no fences and had seen no posting we did not realize that we were on private property. Again I pointed out to him that we were unarmed and could cause him no harm and had no such intentions.

The man told me to shut up and said I talked too much. Then he smiled at me in such a way that it made the hair on the back of my neck rise. He glanced over at his brother and then back at me and told me that he didn't truck with no southern white trash or niggers either. His brother laughed and bobbed his head in agreement. Moreover, since we had seen fit to make ourselves at home on his property without his consent then we were trespassers as well, and these days trespassers could be shot and hardly an eyebrow raised. The brother verified that he was right, that was all very true, very true and added that for all they knew we could even be spies.

By this time I was near panic and in utter disbelief of what I was hearing. They were deliberately twisting the circumstance into something it wasn't, making it sinister and ugly. I protested that we were nothing of the sort and were indeed only enroute to St. Louis to obtain your release from prison. The man with the rifle warned me once more to shut my mouth before he shut it for me, and pointed the rifle at me to prove his sincerity. I quieted, hardly daring to breathe. I had a feeling of dread in the pit of my stomach, my mouth was dry, and my heart was beating so loudly I thought he could surely hear it. We were at their mercy, and I felt it was a virtue neither man possessed. I glanced at Belle, who was warily watching the man with the rifle, then at Joseph, who was quietly watching each man in turn.

After what seemed an eternity the man spoke up again, informing us that he had made his decision. He didn't figure us for spies, he said, because any woman who would attempt that kind of trip with only a couple of niggers and no guns didn't have enough sense to be a spy. Of course, he added, my story was most likely a lie anyway. But being a reasonable man, he would just take his payment and leave us for the night. If we were off his property by daylight, he wouldn't shoot us for trespassing.

Feeling even closer to panic now, I told him we had no money. He looked down at the ground and appeared to be considering this for a moment before he spat in the fire and the looked up at me with that same smile. "Then we'll just take the horse," he said. Still staring and grinning, he leaned toward me and asked if I had any objections. Unable to speak, I merely shook my head. Then he turned to his brother and nodded, and the brother untied Rusty from the back of the cart and led her around behind him. As the men backed away from our campsite the one with the rifle reminded us loudly that they would be back at daylight to see that we were gone. Then they left with Rusty, looking back every few steps to see that we did not attempt to stop them. I heard one of them laughing as they disappeared into the woods.

Had I not been sitting, my knees would surely have given way under me. I felt sick and weak, utterly violated, and absolutely helpless. The could easily have shot us, and who would ever know or even care about it if they did? I have been so naïve as to fear the Yankee soldiers as the enemy and never to even consider civilians being our enemies as well. For the first time I realized exactly how vulnerable we were. Anyone with a gun could impose whatever their will on us, even to take our lives, and we could not protect ourselves or stop them. No matter our virtues or intentions, we were the enemy here. We were nothing.

I looked at Belle and Joseph, feeling as though I was looking up from the bottom of a deep, dark pit. What madness had I dragged them in to? Joseph looked at me and finally spoke, asking me if I was all right. The first words to come to my mind and pass my lips were "I'm so sorry, Joseph." I dropped my head, tears stinging my eyes. Fear, frustration, anger. It was only then that I realized I was shaking. Joseph crossed to Belle and me and sat down between us, putting his arm around Belle. "I could only have taken one of them with my knife," he answered. Squeezing my eyes shut I couldn't help a small sob. I didn't even want to imagine what would have happened had it come to that.

Joseph told me to look at him. Taking a deep breath I did as he asked and quietly, calmly, he spoke, telling me that it was not my doing. He and Belle knew the trip would be dangerous, they discussed it, but in the end we all had to make it regardless of the danger. It was your only chance. If your wounds didn't kill you, then infection could; if not infection, the winter in prison almost certainly would. We couldn't just leave you there if there was any chance of our getting you out and bringing you home. But we had to walk through a war to get to you and we had just seen a glimpse of it. Though the battles are being fought south of us, the war is here, too. Until it ends, it is everywhere.

He patted my hand and rose. I asked him what we were going to do now without Rusty. He smiled and shrugged and answered that we would pull the cart ourselves. With the reins and traces he could make a harness, and two of us could pull it easily. I took him at his word, but told him not to cut the reins because, so help me, at the first opportunity we were going to steal another horse. Without looking up at me he asked me when I last saw a horse walking about loose, or for that matter, a cow. And, Augustus, he was right. Nowhere on our entire trip could I remember seeing a single horse or cow grazing in a field. Being such a common sight I took it for granted and never noticed its absence. Even though ours had been taken early in the war, I assumed the Yankees only took southern horses and cattle. Evidently the Yankees used northern ones as well. Joseph was right, the war was everywhere.

Joseph went quietly to work, telling Belle and me to get some sleep while we could. He would wake us so that we could leave well before daylight. None of us relished the thought of facing our hosts a second time. Belle and I did indeed sleep for a while, and Joseph kept watch the rest of the night.

Gently waking us perhaps an hour before daylight, Joseph had everything in readiness for us to leave. We did not take time for anything to eat, deciding to stop later when it seemed safer. Joseph and I pulled first. He had fashioned a strap between the forward braces of the cart, padded with a quilt. He added two large loops to the strap. We pushed against the strap with the loop around the back of the neck and under one arm, holding on to the brace with our outside hand. It pulled more easily than I anticipated, for which I was grateful as we were not yet halfway to St. Louis. We left at as quick a pace as we dared in the darkness and never saw any further signs of our hosts, for which I was even more grateful.

By dawn we were passing through Hamburg Landing, still traveling as quickly as we could. Though nothing was said I'm sure we all had in mind that the two men might be there or may have spoken of us to someone there. We encountered no one and the little town was behind us before the sun was fully above the horizon.

With my fear more under control now the anger took over. I realize that we were fortunate to have only lost Rusty, but that did not lessen my feeling. Being held at gunpoint and threatened in such a manner for no justifiable reason, feeling that my life could be ended in a moment at this stranger's whim while I was helpless to stop him invoked in me an impotent rage. Rage that such acts are casually perpetrated and yet we call ourselves a civilized society. What a thin and fragile veneer our so-called "civilization" is over total anarchy and chaos! We go through life abiding by the rule of law and expecting others to as well, then suddenly find ourselves at the mercy of those who don't. It's difficult for me to comprehend how little those people realize, or even care, how their deeds impact the lives of their victims. Sometimes the perpetrators are caught and punished. But the deed, and the damage, once done, cannot be undone. Just as words, once spoken, cannot be unspoken. I know that life is not fair, Augustus. What I don't understand is why I keep expecting it to be.

We walked perhaps two hours and Belle changed places with Joseph. She and I cajoled him in to riding in the back of the cart to rest, as he had not had any sleep. He refused at first but finally relented, he said, to give his ears a rest, but only after we promised to wake him if we encountered anyone on the road. He slept until we stopped for lunch.

During lunch we decided to alter our routine slightly and now travel thus; starting before daybreak we have a cold breakfast, then walk until midday when we stop for lunch, doing our cooking then. We rest a little longer than previously at this stop, then we continue until dark, not making our camp until we have its cover. We watch vigilantly to assure ourselves that we have not been followed and we're careful with our campfire, even shielding it with our cart. It has worked well; walking the two additional hours has helped us to make better progress, even without

Rusty. We are, however, quite ready for our rest when we take it.

The land changes past Hamburg Landing, becoming even rougher and very rocky, though the road is good. It is quite sparsely populated and I am relieved, as we have less chance of encountering anyone on the road. We have had no further trouble since Rusty was stolen. Tonight we have camped south of Liberty, but I fear it will be mid-morning before we pass through town, and that makes me apprehensive.

It seems though, if anything, I am even more determined to reach you, Darling, than before. The nights grow cool now and it makes me anxious for your welfare. Joseph and Belle feel it, too, and they are as anxious as I. So we press on. Though I am fearful, I can only believe that my fear of losing you is stronger than my fear of what may lay ahead on the road between us. And so, while I live and breathe, Augustus, it won't stop me from reaching you.

Ever closer,
Rebecca

My Darling,   23 September 1864

Four more days are past, and they bring me ever closer to you. The perplexing quality of time is that it can pass so quickly and so slowly simultaneously. Our days are full and pass readily, yet it seems that the trip has taken us ever so long. Steadily, though, we progress, and tonight are camped about eight miles north of Fort Chartres. If we are able to continue at our present rate we shall reach you within five days.

The past few days have been largely uneventful, for which I am thankful. To be fair it is true that most of the people we pass do no more than cast a curious glance our way, not seeming to want to engage us any more than we would them. But knowing well that there are those who would gladly cause us harm keeps us vigilant and leery of all whom we pass. I am still anxious, my dear, but I feel myself growing more hopeful and lighter of heart, almost daring to believe we will conclude our journey and find you recovering well and waiting for us.

I must tell you that Joseph has surprised me once again with his resourcefulness. The man has talents I had never imagined him having, though I have a feeling that you may be aware of this particular talent and will find the story amusing.

Last night we camped about a mile south of Fort Chartres, stopping about an hour before sunset at Joseph's suggestion. This departure from our new routine made me a little uneasy, but I didn't protest. Knowing the fort was close by, I assumed that Joseph just preferred passing it in the morning instead of so close to darkness.

He pointed out a suitable spot in some trees around the side of a hill from the road, then dropped behind to check that no one had followed us while Belle and I pulled the cart to our site. As I said, camping so close to the Fort did add to my unease and I finally mentioned it to Belle, but she only shrugged in response. We situated our campsite and started supper while waiting for Joseph to rejoin us. Having a little more daylight we decided to cook a meal.

Belle worked and hummed, seeming neither worried nor inclined to conversation. When supper was ready and Joseph still had not returned, my feeling of unease grew stronger and again I mentioned it to Belle. Once again she shrugged it off and replied that he must just be scouting around. She didn't look at me when she answered, and I knew very well that something was afoot, and felt that Belle knew exactly what it was. I was on the verge of confronting her once again when Joseph came into sight, coming around the hill from the north. He walked into camp and, giving Belle a wink, told us that supper smelled real fine and he was mighty hungry.

While we ate I asked Joseph if he had found anything to cause concern on his scouting trip. He replied that all seemed quiet and I caught his glance at Belle. Bemused, I was left with no choice but to wait the scenario out and see what happened. We passed the remainder of the meal with small talk, my curiosity growing. Whatever it was, it seemed to amuse Belle and Joseph. They could hardly look at me and were barely able to contain themselves.

Shortly after supper, just after dark, Belle and I were cleaning up when Joseph rose and stretched and then announced that he was going for a walk. Never had he done this before! I asked him where he was to walk, and why, and did he not think it too dangerous to be strolling about when he stopped me, holding up his hands and chuckling. He assured me that he would be fine and there was no cause for worry. He said there was no one anywhere about to cause us harm, and that we should just go on to sleep and not wait up for him. Then he simply turned and left.

I stared after him a few moments, exasperated and incredulous. Then I turned on Belle, and, a little more loudly than I intended, demanded to know what was going on. Bells put a finger to her lips; she couldn't stop herself from laughing. Hands on my hips, I waited for her to calm herself. When she finally quieted she assured me that everything was fine, Joseph was merely going to get us a horse. I asked her where he had found a horse and she answered, why, at the Yankee fort! Shocked and frightened, I told her that he must have taken complete leave of his senses to try to steal a horse from a fort full of Yankees, and we must catch him and stop him before he got himself shot and us with him. Shaking her head, she told me that I did not understand. He was going to win the horse. Still not understanding, I just stared blankly at her. Giggling now, Belle threw out her fist, opening her fingers and managed, "Roll the bones!"

Augustus, my chin almost hit the ground. I was completely dumbfounded. I never even knew that Joseph gambled, and certainly couldn't picture him throwing dice with the Yankees! Belle was laughing again. Shaking my head now I told her that I was absolutely certain that he had lost his senses and it would serve him right if they threw him in lockup. She smiled and shrugged, but said that he would nonetheless return with a horse. Joseph had not yet returned when it was time to retire, so we went on to sleep.

We awoke just as the darkness was beginning to lighten, and still Joseph had not returned. Alarmed, I looked to see what Belle made of it, but she appeared unconcerned. I decided that this must not be a new experience for her. Having nothing to do but wait, we prepared breakfast and ate, saving Joseph's portion for him.

Afterward Belle had me sit while she prepared another mustard plaster for me. She frets over my cough and I have little choice but to submit to her care. The plasters have done little for my cough, but they do help me breathe more easily. When Belle was finished with her nursing duties we struck camp and packed the cart. Then we sat and waited.

It was fully light when we finally saw Joseph coming around the hill leading, not a horse, but a mule! But that's not entirely accurate, for he was not leading her – she was following him! There was no rope. Belle and I just looked at each other and laughed aloud.

When Joseph and his new friend reached us I rose and, shaking a finger at him, attempted to give him a severe tongue lashing for pulling such a foolhardy stunt and half scaring the life out of me. He tried his best to look contrite but he was just too proud of himself. I gave up the lecture and just shook my head and smiled. Quickly he ate his breakfast and then went about taking our harness apart and putting the reins and traces aright.

The mule is older and a little swaybacked, but she is of good size and seems strong and healthy. She is peculiar in that she follows Joseph around like a puppy. If he turns his back on her she will nose him gently between the shoulder blades to claim his attention. She seems quite content as long as he is close to her and facing her. Belle and I find this amusing and have teased him mercilessly ever since. I call her Shadow.

Once ready to leave we decided that we could all ride in the cart as Shadow could easily pull us. Belle and Joseph sat on the seat and I got in the back. And Shadow wouldn't budge. Joseph clucked, whistled, and finally slapped her hindquarters with the reins, all to no avail. She refused to move. He got down and walked around in front of her. She pulled forward. Joseph walked a few steps, so did Shadow. Then he walked back around her and got into the cart again. She wouldn't move. Joseph told Belle to get down and see if Shadow would follow her. Belle got down and started walking and, lo and behold, Shadow followed. Then Joseph told me to try. I did, with the same result. The silly mule refuses to move on her own, but will follow us! Finally having solved the riddle of Shadow we started off, Joseph in the lead. Once started, she is a good traveler.

As we approached Fort Chartres I saw two sentries in the tower above the gate watching us. They were pointing at us. My heart started to race and I felt the familiar knot of fear in the pit of my stomach. Surely they intended to accuse us of stealing the mule. Then as we drew nearer I could see that they were laughing. Just as we pulled abreast of the tower one of them leaned over and shouted to Joseph, "I see you figured out she's a follower and not a leader!" Joseph threw up a hand with a laugh and we passed on by, the sentries still laughing behind us.

This afternoon we stopped again at yet another abandoned farm, looking to see what we might find in the garden. We dug out a few potatoes and turnips and found some late squash. Coupled with our late start we made only nine or ten miles, but all told it was a good day.

I asked Joseph at supper if he thought those Yankees were still laughing at us. He reckoned that they may be, but said he suspected that he would have the last laugh. With a sly grin he stood, put his hand in his pocket, and brought out gold coins. Fifty dollars in gold! Little wonder he was so pleased with himself. He said he didn't think we would have any difficulty paying our fare to cross the river at St. Louis. Thus, Augustus, your father's pocket watch is safe, we'll spend the Yankees' gold. They probably stole it anyway.

Only a few more days, my love, and I shall reach you at last. I can count them now on one hand. So close that I can almost feel your touch, almost hear the sound of your voice. So close to you, where I belong.

Good night, Love,
Rebecca

Augustus,   27 September 1864

As I write tonight we are camped some five miles south of Illinoistown. Tomorrow will at last bring me to you, Darling, or will prove my journey a fool's errand for which I have paid dearly. I have written to this point of our journey and our experiences, the amusing and the difficult. What I must write now seems impossible to me yet; I don't know that I have the words. These meager words, these phrases and sentences now feel empty and meaningless and completely inadequate in relating the import or emotion of what I must relate. But somehow I will find the words and tell you what has happened, Augustus, because I must, if I have the strength left in me.

We had two good days' travel after I last wrote. We were in good spirits and hopeful, knowing that we were a mere two days from St. Louis and you, the end of our journey in sight. The evening of the second day Joseph picked a site perhaps an hour before dark, as he wanted to go down to the river and try to catch some fish for supper. His occasional good luck has been a welcome change from our usual fare. As Belle and I started some vegetables he tied Shadow so she wouldn't follow him. He took his pole from the cart and headed toward the river. Shadow turned and watched him leave, then stood quietly, staring at the spot where he disappeared down the steep bank.

It was only a short time later, still well light, and the vegetables just starting to boil when Shadow shook her head and pawed the ground. Belle and I stopped talking and looked toward the river where we saw Joseph walking toward us, followed by two men. They both wore homespuns and black felt hats; one wore a brown jacket and the other wore a tan jacket. Both were disheveled and filthy. They were not smiling or talking and we could tell from Joseph's posture that something was amiss.

We stood without saying a word and watched. As they drew closer we could see that the man in the brown jacket was holding one of Joseph's arms behind his back. Walking into the campsite the man pulled Joseph to a stop and then fiercely twisted his arm up further behind his back, making him wince with pain. With his other hand he brought a knife up to Joseph's throat. Joseph managed to tell us they wanted food.

I took a step forward and the man pressed the knife closer to Joseph's throat. I stopped and begged him to please let Joseph go, telling him that we would be glad to give them our dinner. Never loosening his grip on Joseph the man said they didn't have time for dinner. He said there might be some men looking for them and they couldn't wait. They had confiscated themselves a boat and two friends of theirs were waiting with it at the river. They had to keep going. I told them they could take our food with them, just please let Joseph go. I told him you were a Confederate captain and we were going to St. Louis to get you out of prison. I told him we were unarmed and could not harm him. Curling his lip he said that he didn't give a good goddamn if I was Robert E. Lee's daughter, on my way to spring the old man himself.

Belle had picked up our vegetable sack and sack of meal and held them out, asking him to let Joseph go now, please. She repeated that we wouldn't cause them any harm. I looked at Joseph and saw the sweat trickle down his temples. I saw the blade of the knife pressing into the skin on the side of his neck and saw one small drop of blood slide slowly down his neck. His breathing was labored. He looked at me, then at Belle. There was no fear in his eyes, only pain and concern. Joseph was concerned for our welfare, Augustus, not his own.

The man with the knife backed away a couple of steps, dragging Joseph with him. He told the man in the tan jacket to get the food. The man grabbed the sacks from Belle then backed away. The man holding Joseph asked me if we had any more food. I told him we had a sack of beans and some apples in the cart and he ordered me to get the sacks, slowly, and set them down to his side. I did as I was told and he ordered me back to where I stood, on the other side of the fire. Moving back I asked once more, please, take the food but just let Joseph go.

Augustus, they were desperate, vile men with dead, soulless eyes. The men who stole Rusty were mean, conniving thieves, but these men were far worse; they were pure evil. I could see that my pleading did not even register with them, and knew they would not give us a moments' consideration. They would just as soon kill us as not with no compunction whatsoever. To them we were nothing.

Then, in a blur, the man with the knife literally hurled Joseph straight at me, right through the campfire. He bent, grabbed the two sacks, and then both men turned and ran. Joseph, trying to catch his balance, stumbled through the fire, knocking over the pot of vegetables, scattering burning wood and embers before landing on his hands and knees in front of Belle and me. Belle cried out and immediately dropped to her knees to help him.

Quickly I glanced toward the men to assure myself they were truly leaving. Still running toward the river brown jacket whooped and yelled to his companion, "Did ya see that?" The other man asked why he did it and he yelled back, "'Cause I felt like it!"

When I looked back down Joseph was on his knees facing Belle, who had her hands on his shoulders as if holding him up. Joseph had one hand to his neck, and from under it the blood ran freely. The front of his shirt was already soaked. His mouth opened and closed but no sound came out. His eyes were wide open in a glazed stare. The blood was bubbling now under his hand. I knelt down with them, and Belle and I carefully laid Joseph down with his head in her lap. I told her I would get the bandages from the cart but she just shook her head. She knew that it was already too late. She just kept repeating his name, "Joseph, Joseph." She held him stroking his face and calling his name as his eyes closed. He convulsed twice and was gone. In less than two minutes, Augustus, Joseph was dead.

Belle wept from her soul. I did not weep, and have not yet, for I fear that if I start I may never be able to stop. The pain is so great that I cannot assimilate it; I cannot yet believe that he is truly gone. Thoughts and images of Joseph crowd my mind, one after another. Quiet, strong, sensitive Joseph. I thought of our baby, Augustus, the little boy we buried just four years ago. Joseph had made his beautiful cradle, and I remember how he cried when he took it up to the attic. I cried then, too, but it was different. I had you to hold me, and later I held you. Now I must be strong for Belle, and there is no one to whom I may turn.

Belle sat holding Joseph until well after dark. I left her only to add wood to the fire. There were no adequate words to speak, so we were silent. When it grew late, I told her that we must cover him and try to sleep. Tenderly she laid him down and covered him, then wrapped herself in her blankets and sat with him. So I did the same. From time to time we would nod off only to awaken in a few minutes to find the nightmare continuing.

In the morning, just yesterday morning, we sat until well after daylight. As gently as I could, I told Belle that we must wash him and bury him. She nodded as tears welled up in her eyes and said that she would wash him. I told her I would dig the grave. First taking the buckets down to the river for water, I found myself watching for the killers even though I knew they were long gone from us. As I knelt and filled the buckets I happened to glance down to my left, and there was Joseph's cane pole lying on the bank, ready with line and hook. The pain seared my heart and very nearly overwhelmed me. I had to put out my hand on the bank to steady myself and closed my eyes tight, fighting to keep my composure. Regaining control after a few minutes, I took the buckets and climbed the bank, leaving the pole behind.

Walking back to the camp I passed Shadow, whom I had completely forgotten, poor thing. She had been so quiet. Perhaps she sensed our loss. I retied her in another spot to give her graze and gave her one of the buckets of water as well. The other bucket I gave to Belle, then I took the shovel from the cart and looked for a suitable spot for Joseph's grave. How could I possibly do this? It seemed as if my mind and body were two separate beings. My body was going about doing what had to be done seemingly without direction from my mind, which was scattered and could not follow a logical train of thought. Instead, it jumped and wandered from one thought to another and back again.

At last I located a nice spot on a little rise free of trees and started to dig. The soil is poor and rocky here, and digging is hard. After a couple of hours I had hardly managed a plot more than two or three inches deep. My strength was almost gone and I realized that we had not eaten anything since the day before at lunch. I knew we had to eat whether we had an appetite for it or not.

Going back to the campsite I found that Belle had cleaned Joseph and even managed to change his blood soaked clothes. He lay on a blanket looking for all the world as if he were only sleeping peacefully. He looked younger. But the ugly, gaping wound on the side of his neck told the jarring truth. Quickly I shifted my gaze. Belle was no longer crying, at least for the moment. She held out her hand to me, palm up, and in it were the gold coins Joseph had won from the Yankees. Amazingly, the killers must not have considered that we may have had any money. I took the coins and tied them into the hem of my skirt.

I told Belle that we must eat something and I would prepare it. Again I took the buckets to the river; this time avoiding the spot where Joseph's fishing pole lay. Back at the campsite, walking past the fire to the cart I saw the spilled vegetables from the night before. I picked up what I could salvage, washed them off and put them back on to boil. Then I checked our supplies. They were running low, only partial sacks each of flour, meal, and beans. Very little was left of the vegetables and apples. Our tins of lard and molasses were almost empty, and the baking soda, powder, and salt were almost gone. I vaguely wondered why the killers didn't take any more than they did, but my mind didn't want to formulate any answers. Frankly, I didn't care. I only knew I was looking at the reality I would have to cope with for now. We would have to resupply before the trip home. At least we had the gold. I would handle that later. For now I added a handful of meal and a little flour to the vegetables. We ate the mush for lunch.

After eating and resting a little I resumed the grave digging. Belle still sat with Joseph, and when I occasionally looked her way I could see that she was talking to him. I didn't think my heart could hurt any worse, but I was wrong. I couldn't even begin to imagine what she was feeling. I tried to concentrate on what I was doing and not look over there again.

Perhaps an hour had passed with my making meager progress when we heard the shouts of men and the noise of horses coming through the trees and underbrush down the riverbank from the north. I walked back to Belle and we stood by Joseph, waiting, neither of us speaking. I don't know that either of us had the energy or forethought to even wonder what would happen next.

Shortly there appeared two men through a break in the trees and then into the clearing. They spotted us almost immediately but remained where they were, sitting on their horses and waiting for their companions. Soon they were joined by two more men, then more, until there were eight. All wore blue uniforms; Yankees. Though we could hear their voices, we could not distinguish their words. Then two of them turned their horses and started toward us while the others waited. I still held my shovel and did not put it down, though I could see that they were well armed. As they neared the campsite I could tell that one was a captain and the other was a private, and I remember feeling some relief that neither was a sergeant.

Stopping just short of the campsite the captain stared, taking in the scene. It was only then that I realized that neither Belle nor I had thought to change our own blood stained clothes. The captain dismounted and, tipping his hat, he gently asked us if we could tell him what had happened here. He said they were looking for four men, renegades, he called them, and wanted to know if they had done this.

Through clenched teeth I told him that the men they were looking for were cold-blooded killers, and they were too late. Nodding his affirmation he allowed me to continue, and continue I did. I told him everything. About the Yankee, about you, the trip, Rusty's being stolen, and the men killing Joseph. It all spilled out, I couldn't stop myself. The fear, the frustration, the anger, the pain were all there. I told him the whole ugly story, and though my voice cracked several times, I did not cry.

The captain listened quietly and carefully until I finished. Then he removed his hat and told us how sorry he was about Joseph. He said he could not right the wrongs done us, but he could help us. Putting out his hand, he asked me for my shovel. I handed it to him and he took it to the private and spoke a few words to him. The private left and rejoined the other men.

While the men the finished digging Joseph's grave the captain sat with Belle and me. He told us he was assigned to the federal arsenal at St. Louis and had volunteered for the search party as some of the men do from boredom and the want to get out of doors for a few days. As there was no hope of catching the killers now, they would be returning to St. Louis. Four of the men he would send on ahead, the other four would escort us and deliver us personally to Major Ayers. He knew the major and respected him highly, saying he was a good and fair man.

The men had plenty of food, which they would freely share with us. If we didn't mind cooking for them, he was sure the men would appreciate our cooking much more than their own, but we needn't feel obligated. Indeed, they would even prepare our meals for us if we so desired, and set up a separate campsite for us. I looked at Belle, who was quiet though she listened carefully. She nodded her agreement, so I told the captain we would cook.

One of the men came over to advise the captain that the grave was ready. And such was Joseph's funeral. Far from home in some nameless place with only Belle and me to mourn him, with seven Yankee soldiers standing uncomfortably by, their captain trying his best to speak the appropriate words for his service. I credit the captain for trying, but the man had never laid eyes on Joseph in life and could never know the person he was. He could not speak to all that Joseph had given in life, all that he had suffered, and the enormity of his loss. He deserved better, Augustus, he gave so much better. Damn this war, damn all of those who perpetuate it, and damn all of those who feed off of it!

With it being dusk when we finished, we stayed one more night; Belle and I finally exhausted enough to sleep. And I dreamed a strange dream. I found myself in the middle of a frozen lake, trying to walk to shore. I was carrying something in a sack. It was heavy but I could not put it down, for there was no one else to carry it. I was so cold, I was overwhelmingly exhausted, and I was almost petrified with fear, Augustus, because with every step I took I could hear the ice cracking. And if the ice gave way I knew I would be lost. But there was nothing for me to do but keep walking, not knowing whether the next step I took would be my last. One step from oblivion. I have never felt so alone and so afraid. I awoke suddenly, shivering, with the sound of ice still cracking in my ears, and my heart pounding. The camp was quiet. The fires were low, and I saw the sentry calmly walking the perimeter on the far side of the soldiers' camp. I got up and went to the cart for another blanket. Eventually I fell asleep again and dreamed no more.

We left this morning, Belle and I riding as one of the soldiers led Shadow, walking his own horse. The captain tells me tonight we will arrive in St. Louis tomorrow. So we shall. I dare not think of what I may find at the end of my journey. I will wait and see, and cope then with whatever I must. I pray for His strength, I have no more of my own. For now I am numb and I prefer it so. Again I am reminded that if I feel the hope and joy, then I must also feel the pain. And sometimes, Augustus, there is just too much pain.

Know that I love you,
Rebecca

My dearest Sister,   1 October 1864

    I fervently hope that this letter finds all of you at home in good health and in good spirits. We arrived in St. Louis only three days ago, our trip being more difficult than I could ever have imagined and taking longer than anticipated. I have taken this earliest opportunity to set out to you some of what has transpired since I last saw you.

    We have found Augustus alive, though he has been terribly wounded. Upon our arrival in St. Louis we went to the Gratiot Street prison where he had been taken. I was escorted directly to Major Ayers, whose direct responsibility is the supervision of this prison. He has been most solicitous and kind, Mary, as far as his capacity will allow. After my trip to Union City he received a wire inquiring about Augustus and followed up on it immediately, only to find him very near death from neglect of treatment.

    The prison is an old slave holding pen; an irony lost on neither the captors nor their prisoners. Filled beyond capacity, the conditions are shocking, and more deplorable than I will here relate. Suffice it to say that no animal we have ever had on the farm has been so ill-treated. I wonder that any man could survive it. The major says he does what he can, but finds little sympathy for his views and has only the barest resources at his disposal.

    There is another prison in St. Louis, the Myrtle Street prison, which was the McDowell Medical College before the war. The Yankees send wounded prisoners there as space allows and it serves as both a prison and a hospital. It, too, is filled past capacity. Even though he was told there were no beds available the major had Augustus put into a wagon and personally accompanied him to the prison so that he would not be turned away. At his insistence they made room for Augustus and the major even remained there until a doctor saw him. The doctor himself is a captured southern officer, Dr. Richard Hawkens of Nashville. He has worked tirelessly with Augustus and the major has monitored his progress quite diligently. Together they have saved his life, Mary.

Speaking at length with the major and Dr. Hawkens I have learned much about Augustus' condition. He was injured by a shell that exploded beneath his horse. He sustained numerous shrapnel wounds, but worse, has a severe concussion resulting in swelling of the brain. The doctor has drilled holes in his skull to relieve fluid and pressure and feels that it has stabilized his condition. He has been unconscious for most of his time here. Even in his periods of consciousness he is seldom lucid.

Listening to the doctor's assessment frightened me and brought innumerable questions to mind. Dr. Hawkens has been endlessly patient with me; answering all of my questions as best as he could, and explained that, in fact, he believed Augustus to be improving. He feels that the swelling may be subsiding as his reflexes are improving, he is less combative, and he rests more quietly. He cannot tell me, however, to what extent Augustus may recover. It is only due to his stout constitution that he has survived thus far, as his taking nourishment is a haphazard occurrence.

Augustus has awakened only four times since my arrival, but has not been lucid. He has not as yet recognized me. He is in a small room with three other men. Dr. Hawkens allows me to sit with him and has shown me how to assist somewhat with his care. I am amazed that he has spent so much time with Augustus as he is so grossly overworked. There is only one other doctor, and each has one assistant. Already I have seen several men here, patients themselves, assisting other patients in need of help. The guards do not participate in the care of the wounded, but they do seem to treat the men humanely for the most part. For want of something to keep her mind and body occupied Belle has been helping the assistants with their patient care, and they all greatly appreciate her calm and efficient manner. At night we sleep on cots in Dr. Hawkens office, and the guards pretend not to notice.

We will of necessity remain here until Augustus is well enough to survive the trip home. Dr. Hawkens cannot give us an answer as to how long that may be, but when pressed guessed that it could be another three to four weeks with good progress, or three to four months otherwise. I can only pray that it not be as arduous as the trip here.

I will, of course, correspond with you regularly as I am assured that my letters will be delivered by Yankee dispatch. I will take advantage of that and anything else I may, as I feel the Yankees are responsible for us being here at all. There is, however, one exception. Dr. Hawkens has tried to treat me with medication for my cough but I have refused it. Medication is in such short supply that there is not enough for the wounded, and I will not take it from them. They have much greater need for it than I. Enough that they feed us. There seems to be sufficient food though the fare is plain and the portions scant.

I have finally overcome my fear of the blue uniform, Mary, for I have learned that it is not the color of the uniform, whether blue or gray, but it is the man wearing it who is to be feared or may be trusted. Even war has its rules of engagement. And there are men on both sides who will disregard them at the expense of the innocent.

As I have told you, Mary, the trip was quite difficult. Inclement weather stopped our progress for a few days, and Rusty was stolen from us. A few days after she was stolen Joseph acquired a mule for us in quite an unusual manner. He won her gambling with the Yankees at Fort Chartres.

Speaking of our dear Joseph, I can no longer put off what I must tell you now. The most heartbreaking news possible, Mary. Our dear Joseph is gone. Only two days out of St. Louis he was killed by two men on the run from the Yankees. They accosted us in our camp and stole a few sacks of food from us. For such meager bounty they killed Joseph, even though we offered no resistance and posed no threat to them. A Yankee patrol showed up the next day looking for them. The captain called them renegades. They were just evil men killing for sport. Men whose lives weren't worth a single hair on Joseph's head. Arriving too late to save Joseph and too late to catch the men, the patrol buried Joseph there in that nameless place, then escorted Belle and me the remainder of the way to St. Louis, and to Augustus.

Belle is devastated. Of late she has been helping with the wounded men, and having something to occupy her thoughts, having some purpose, may help her in a way I cannot. She goes through the motions and does them well, but her heart is not in it. I fear that she will never recover from her loss, and I can understand that. They spent a lifetime together, and loved and respected one another. They were part of each other. That cannot be replaced. I don't know how any of us will manage without him, Mary, and most of all I dread telling Augustus. Belle and Joseph were with his father before us, and they have been a part of his life since the beginning. He will be devastated as well. I know that Samson and Lizbeth will be heartbroken, too. Samson looked on Joseph like a father. Joseph was always very proud of that, and loved them as much as they loved him.

For the time, dearest Sister, I feel nothing. Joseph's death is a blow I have yet to feel, and Augustus' condition leaves me still unknowing whether I will ever have again the man I love so dearly. I do not know whether it is death trying to cheat me or whether it is life itself. Only time will provide my answers, and I must wait them out. So we will remain here, Belle and I, until I have those answers. I do hope that you will inform Charles and Alma of the news thus far, and please express to them my best regards. I am so sorry that it falls to you to have to relate to everyone the news of Joseph's death.

I will keep you abreast of Augustus' progress, and we will remain hopeful that good news will be forthcoming soon regarding his condition. Of course, I will write you before we begin our journey home. Let us hope that it will be soon.

You may write me here, Mary, using the envelopes I am enclosing with my letter. They are addressed and marked for official business and therefore will be delivered post haste. Just have Samson take them to the Yankee headquarters in Troy. I am so anxious for news of you all there at home, so please answer as quickly as you can. I would love to hear news of how little Shane is doing. How are you doing yourself? Tell me any news of Samson and Lizbeth, of Charles and Alma and the children. Belle and I miss you all so terribly. We look forward to your letter.

Take good care, sweet Sister, kiss Shane for me,
Rebecca

My darling Sister,   1 November 1864

As I read your letter, dear Sister, you cannot imagine how overwhelmed with gratitude and relief I was. I have carried my guilt over the Yankee with me for so long now in the dark fringes of my consciousness, where it has been festering. Finally it is all out in the open and I feel cleansed of it. I was glad to hear that Samson and Lizbeth sat down and related the whole story to you, Charles, and Alma. But you must know that the decision was mine alone, Mary, and the responsibility.

I will not apologize for acting as I did. I struggled at the time with my own ambivalent feelings of loyalty, revenge, and doing the right and Christian thing. But I can tell you with the utmost sincerity that it was never my intention to hurt anyone, least of all you, Charles, Alma, or Augustus. If I have done so inadvertently then I do offer my most humble and sincere apologies for that.

I had no way of knowing at the time just how far-reaching my actions would be; indeed I never even contemplated that particular perspective. I only knew that I must do as my heart dictated because, ultimately, I must live with my own conscious. With all honesty I can tell you that my frame of mind of late has been one of utter disgust and weariness of the war. I could not bring myself to become an active participant in the mindless, and seemingly endless, carnage, destruction, and waste. Had the Yankee posed a threat to us I would have acted much differently with no compunction whatsoever, but such was not the case.

The one time I spoke to him I noticed that he wore a wedding band. I thought of you, Alma, and me. I thought of some unknown woman hoping for some news of her husband, awaiting his homecoming. For all I know he may be a father as well, I did not ask. But he was not a bad man, and I knew that deep inside. It made me heartsick, and I knew that I could not bear any more weight of it all. Thus he was spared, not from noble intentions on my part, but from weakness.

Since arriving in St. Louis and meeting Major Ayers I see him often here at the hospital. He follows Augustus' progress most diligently, and frequently checks on Belle and me as well. Not long after I arrived he asked me to relate to him the whole story, so I told it to him. When I finished, he asked me what I intended to tell Augustus. Taking a deep breath and hesitating only slightly, I told him I must tell Augustus the truth, and then live with whatever the consequence.

Quietly he asked me how I thought Augustus might react to the truth. Taken aback by his boldness I asked him why he would ask me such a question. Somewhat abashed by his own forward behavior he nonetheless pressed on, telling me that he thought perhaps he could help, and wanted my consent to speak to Augustus about the matter. Mary, I have no idea what possessed me, it was plain that he was truly sincere and I am not a vindictive person, but I just couldn't resist making him squirm a little. I can only think that perhaps I was mildly offended by his brashness in questioning me about so personal a matter. In my most straightforward manner I asked him exactly what he hoped to accomplish by speaking to Augustus. He was, after all, the enemy, the captor, and he didn't even know Augustus. The major acknowledged that all of that was very true, but added that he felt he may be able to speak to Augustus as a fellow officer. He wanted to be sure that Augustus understood that my saving the Yankee's life was the very thing that saved his. He reminded me that I had saved a dear friend of his and that he was in my debt. With a self-conscious smile he told me he thought he could do a better job of presenting the story in its best light with the added weight of his perspective. At least I had the grace to feel just a little ashamed of myself. I nodded my consent and thanked him for his concern.

The major told me to send word to him at whatever time I was ready. I told him that I would consult Dr. Hawkens for his opinion as to when Augustus had sufficiently recovered to discuss the matter with him. I only warned him that I wanted to tell Augustus the truth before he started asking questions, for I would not lie to him about how I came to make the trip to St. Louis. As he has so much improved in a fairly short time, I feel that discussion is near.

I have already broken the news of Joseph's death to him, with Belle at my side, and he took it quite badly. He said he felt responsible and was inconsolable for some two days and seemed to regress in his progress somewhat. Belle sat with him for hours, talking to him. She absolutely would not allow him to blame himself and finally calmed him. She told him the story of Shadow, and Joseph rolling dice with the Yankees and taking their gold. Together they even smiled through their tears. She told Augustus that's how she wanted him to remember Joseph. Time, she said, will eventually dull the pain and leave us with the good memories, and if she could endure it, then he could, too. With tears in his eyes he nodded and promised her he would.

It was hardly a week ago that Dr. Hawkens decided that Augustus was ready to hear the story of the Yankee. As I had with Charles, I spoke honestly about my actions and about my emotions and motivations, making no apologies for them. Augustus listened quietly, gravely, to both the major and I until we were finished. He closed his eyes for a moment, then opened them and took my hand. Looking me straight in the eye he told me that he knew very well that I would act on my convictions, no matter what the situation, no matter how difficult. Having such faith in me he would not ill judge my decision or my actions. He felt that there was nothing to forgive and, after all, as the major pointed out, my saving the Yankee's life had saved his as well.

So, dear Sister, worthy or not, I am forgiven, and I am most grateful for it. For all of you mean all the world to me. It is quite profound for me to realize that it is the love we share that gives us the ability to accept each other wholly and unconditionally; and thus the ability to give one another whatever is needed, be it comfort, encouragement, or even forgiveness. How fortunate I am to have the love of all of you!

So now I share with you the greatest of news with a joyous heart, my dear little Sister. We are coming home at last! Dr. Hawkens has finally consented today to discharge Augustus. He is amazed at his recovery and often shakes his head, telling Augustus how fortunate he is.

His health is so much improved. He still sleeps almost ten hours a day, but stays awake for much longer periods now. The headaches are much less frequent and not nearly as severe, his hands hardly tremble at all, so that now he may feed himself. Though he walks with a pronounced limp Dr. Hawkens feels that he is fortunate to walk at all considering badly his foot and ankle were shattered. But I am most thankful that his mind and spirit have returned almost completely, and intact. There are details he has lost, lines from some of his favorite poems, for instance, but his thought processes and disposition are the Augustus we all know. Dr. Hawkens believes that his memory for detail may yet improve. He has been through so much, Mary; he has literally fought his way back from death's door. The doctor says he has recovered mostly from sheer force of will, telling me that he has seen many men with lesser wounds who never recovered. Shaking his head in wonder, he told me that this is the part of medical practice that is outside a doctor's domain.

Augustus and I talk almost constantly while he is awake, so much so that the men tease him and tell him to go back to sleep that they may have some peace and quiet. So we lower our voices like naughty children, and then invariably wind up laughing or giggling over something and disturbing them anyway! It may sound strange that we would behave so. I think that we're trying hard to make up for all of the precious time we have lost. Perhaps it is just that we both realize how very fortunate we are to have found each other again that makes us so deliriously happy. So many have lost so much, as we all well know.

I have told him the news of the farm, and the news of you and little Shane. He sends his sincerest condolences, Mary, and wishes he could have known Phillip. He is so pleased that you both will be with us, and he looks forward to getting to know Shane. I think they will share a special bond, Shane having lost his father, and Augustus having lost his son. Each is a godsend to the other.

This morning Major Ayers stopped by to congratulate Augustus on the good news; he had already spoken to Dr. Hawkens. The major offered to furnish us a wagon and a mule (one that doesn't have to be led!) and supplies enough to see us home. There is a Yankee transport leaving for Cairo next week and we may travel with them if we wish. Augustus has agreed to this, being mindful of his condition and our safety. They travel long hours, but that will only serve to bring us home more quickly. A good trip will see us home by Thanksgiving, Mary, and would that not be appropriate? I think so!

Belle sends her love to all of you. She is a little more herself of late, though still very quiet. She has kept herself busy here and I believe it has helped her. Her nursing skills have been well appreciated and I think will be sorely missed. The weather has been cold and rainy, though there has been no snow. I know Belle's rheumatism bothers her, but of course she never complains of it. My cough has been aggravated by the weather as well, and Dr. Hawkens, Belle, and Augustus all fret over me. I have continued to refuse any medication until today. Major Ayers brought some to me and, telling me that it was Yankee medicine, begged me to take it, promising that I would not be depriving any prisoner. I suspect it may have been a ruse concocted by the major and the doctor, but they badgered me so that I finally relented and took it. I hope that it makes them feel better!

We are so glad to hear from you the news of home and to know that all of you are doing well. It always lifts Augustus' spirits to hear what Samson has done or what he may have planned. He is so anxious now to get back home so that he may get as much work done as possible before spring planting. Augustus wonders if Charles plans to rebuild his store and wants to help if that is the case. Such talk for a man who can only yet walk a dozen paces! I have no doubt that he will see his plans realized. He never mentions the influence of the war on any part of our future. As he is done with it now it is as if it no longer exists. That is out of his normal character, but I feel that he will deal with whatever reality he finds when we arrive home. To be fair, none of us know what each day will bring.

I imagine that you must have to keep a sharp eye on Shane now that he is crawling, I'm sure there is no stopping him! I'm happy to hear that little Charles and Althea enjoy him so. They will be wonderful companions for him as he grows.

Please relate to everyone our best regards and the wonderful news. Know that we love you and miss you all terribly, and that we are counting the days until we see the end of our journey and are back home and together again.

Your loving sister,
Rebecca

My Darling,   5 November 1864

As I sit by your side watching you sleep I am, from long habit, writing to you. It has been my way of keeping you close to me, almost as if I am talking to you, though in reality I have in fact been talking to myself. But I have come to enjoy it and even to take comfort in it, my pretense that I am sharing with you, somehow connecting with you. So I have kept writing, even after the letters I sent started coming back to me. I never stopped writing them; I only stopped sending them. Even so, I hope this to be my last letter, for it is a poor substitute for your real presence. This time I take up my pen to write the words I want you to remember. You know well that I believe in saying the good things. Put down thus they will not fade or grow dim with memory. You will have them whenever you wish; if you think of me and grow nostalgic, if you are lonely and want for comfort, or perhaps even if you feel lost and seek direction. This, Darling, is my final soliloquy.

You are sleeping peacefully now and it is still startling to me to look over and see you there, right beside me. I'm quite sure I've reached over to touch you at least a thousand times these past weeks, just to make sure it is truly you and not some fantasy I have yearned into being. It's as if seeing you is not enough; I must touch you as well. Time and again I have felt my heart catch in my throat as I realize I truly have you back.

When I first arrived here I sat with you for four days, watching and waiting, wondering if your spirit had been as badly wounded as your body. I talked to you almost ceaselessly, of our lives, the farm, the news since you have been gone; I told you your favorite stories, recited your favorite poems, held your hand and stroked your cheek trying to reach you, to find you and bring you back. Our paths have brought us back together, my love, in this sad place in this strange city and I do not believe it is all for naught. I have so much more to give, Augustus, and if it is only kept inside and not given then I will have wasted my life. And you have so much more ahead of you. You are so young and strong, so loved and needed.

And then at last you awoke, and you were lucid. As I sat on the edge of your bed, I put my hand to your cheek, and you looked at me with such intensity. I saw the confusion in your face, I could see you struggling, searching somewhere deep in your mind to find the connection you felt in your heart. Then I saw the recognition dawn in your eyes, and you spoke my name. It was a question, but I was there to verify the truth. You reached up then and touched my face and repeated my name, a statement this time. And finally, after so long a time, your embrace. I felt your warmth again, and your love; it filled my heart. I felt the strength and comfort I had missed so terribly. It was all still there. I did not ever want to ever again leave that embrace, but I knew I must get you to eat something before you went back to sleep. You ate a little and indeed dropped off again to sleep, whispering my name as you closed your eyes. It was the sweetest sound I have ever heard, my Darling. And I knew then that I had you back, body and soul. I saw it in your eyes; I felt it in your embrace. I knew in my heart that you would recover, you would be all right.

With the crisis past, finally on solid ground, the strain of these past years overcame me and my defenses crumbled, as I knew they eventually would. All of the feelings I had held at bay came flooding over me all at once; I could no longer hold them back. Quietly I slipped out of your room and went to Dr. Hawkens office, praying that he was not there. Thank goodness he wasn't. As I sat in his chair, my arms resting on his desk, I laid my head on my arms and wept as I never have before.

I thought of Major Ayers shaking my hand the day we met, telling me he had never met a more courageous or determined woman. His statement mystified me. I don't understand how he could reach such a conclusion. If he could but see me now he would know how wrong he was. Courageous? I hardly remember the day I haven't lived in fear. Fear of Yankees, fear of not having enough to eat, and, worst of all, fear of losing you. Determined? I did what must be done. I had no other choice. All of the decisions of the last three years had to be made. How many times have I wished I could just give up, or run away, or defer to someone else? Countless times. So after all, Augustus, how courageous and determined have I really been?

I wept for the loss and deprivation we have suffered; for Phillip and Joseph lost to us now forever, both guiltless in acts of war but both taken by it; for Charles loss of his arm and part of his spirit to the war. I wept for the fear and the pain and the anger, for the loss of our peace and well-being; the injustices suffered with no recourse; lifetimes built and torn asunder, then trampled on for years over and again until there is finally no chance for recovery. For all of us touched by this war have been wounded; those wounds are deep and far-reaching.

I wept from the exhausting enormity of it all; the death, the waste, the blood, the evil, and the destruction. All of it unimaginable. Incomprehensible. Unexplainable. Unbearable. And unnecessary. But all too real. Too real.

Finally I wept with relief. In the rubble of our lives we have at least found each other again. Not to pick up our old lives, to be sure, but a chance to have another kind of life together, whatever we make of it, and most of those we love still with us. And then I wept for hope and joy. That enduring hope of the human soul that I thought I had lost is still there after all, and will sustain me as it always has, whether or not I was aware of it. And the pure joy of having you back again, born of my love. It feels almost as if it has been dormant for many a season and is now coming back to life. Like my morning glories, it has survived and blooms again.

Done with my weeping, my pain and tears behind me, I finally regained a semblance of composure and returned to sit by your side. Belle had stopped in to check on you and was sitting by your side as you slept. One glance told her that I had finally succumbed to my feelings and she rose quickly and came to me, a look of deep concern on her face. I smiled to show her I was all right now, and then told her that you had at last awakened and had recognized me. Overwhelmed, unable to speak, she hugged me and stroked my hair. Rocking me, comforting me, and praising the Lord. She herself even shed a few tears, as if she had not shed enough already. Bless her, even in her mourning, she still thinks of others.

Since that day your health has steadily improved and you have recovered well, far better than Dr. Hawkens ever expected. We have discovered each other again, and found that the connection we have always shared is still intact. We have talked so much of so many things, and we have shared comfortable silence when no words were needed.

There is but one thing left untold that I must find a way to tell you. As you recovered and grew stronger I could feel myself growing weaker. I have driven myself for so long, but after the rest of being in one place as long as we have I could deny it no longer. I spoke with Dr. Hawkens, and after some tests he confirmed two days ago what we both had suspected; I have tuberculosis. He tells me that with good care I have at least six months, possibly a year. I have made him promise to say nothing; I will find a way to tell you once we return home. We will be leaving the day after tomorrow, the joyous occasion made bittersweet to me because I know our time to be short.

I feel an incredible sadness that we will not see long years ahead of us. Selfishly, I intend to fight as long as I am able; I do not want to give you up. But we have already come so close to losing each other and I am so grateful to have you back at all that I do not feel angry. We have lost three precious years; we haven't the time left now to waste on anger. I feel that whatever time we have left we will spend it well. I had already made a vow that if I ever got you back, I would live the rest of our time together so that I would have no regrets. So I shall, but it will be a shorter time than I expected. How well we know that every book, every poem, every story has its end. And so our story, too, will soon see its end. What you must remember, Augustus, is that it has been a wonderful story and it has a happy ending. The importance of life is not how long it is lived, but how well it is lived. We have had a good life, Darling, and I believe we have lived it well.

You are the finest man I have ever known. One of impeccable character, good and fair, respectful of others, generous, intelligent, sensitive, and of the best humor. I have always held you in the highest esteem, of which you are most worthy. I have always found you fascinating; I am still in awe of you. My pulse still quickens when you come into my view. I have loved you truly, Augustus, and I have tried my best to love you well. Nothing has been more important to me than to make you feel loved, happy, and content. I have always been mindful of what may please you and how I might accomplish it; whether it be a new book I think you might enjoy, a few special words to lift you up if you feel low, a back rub if you have overworked, or making love to you the right way at the right time. Anything that would show you how much I love and respect you, how much I value and appreciate you.

In all things I strive to do my best, to be my best, because you inspire that in me, Augustus. That is part of the magic. If I have succeeded in my life's endeavor it is because you have enabled me to do so. And therein lays the rest of the magic. I know that you have loved me truly, and you have loved me well. You have never made me feel less than the most valuable person in your life. Your love, respect, and faith lift me up from being ordinary to become extraordinary. Knowing that my wants and needs are anticipated, met, and exceeded gives me implicit faith and trust in you. Being secure in your love frees me to give you mine wholly and unconditionally, just as you give me yours. That is why it has worked so well for us. We take care of each other with love, yes, but also with equal respect.

Like puzzle pieces we fit together. Differently on different days and with different moods, but we always fit. Separately we are whole, but together we are complete. I felt from the beginning that our souls truly connected. The feeling was right and certain, like we recognized each other, knew each other's souls. And I do believe that is why we have loved as we do. Perhaps we were blessed with this intensity because our time together was to be so brief. I don't know the answer. But I do know that we have both been humbly appreciative and grateful for it, for we both realize how rare and precious it is, and how fortunate we were to find it. And it is ours to share for a little longer.

I look forward now, Augustus, with purpose. There is so much that awaits us for the time we have left to us. The farm needs so much work, and the house. Samson is so enthusiastic to see it done. You will meet little Shane, who needs you to teach him. You will be reunited with your brother and the two of you will share a new depth of understanding of each other that you have never had before.

You will read to me again, we will have our evenings on the porch, and our walks. We will have a new depth of understanding and appreciation, too. We will again have our beautiful moments. But what I look forward to most of all, Augustus, is the day when, having recovered, you will put your arms around me again. You will tell me that everything will be all right, and I will believe it. And with your arms around me I will lay my head on your chest, close my eyes, and lean on you, and you will hold me up.

With love and hope,
Rebecca

They rocked in silence, the old woman giving the girl time to absorb it all. The sun had dipped toward the river, taking its warmth with it, and the old woman pulled her sweater closer around her. She glanced at the girl and saw a tear slide down her cheek and heard her sniff. Yes, she was the sensitive one, but it was one of the traits that endeared her so to the old woman. She pulled a tissue out of the box she had brought out with her, handed it to the girl, then gently rubbed her arm and gave it a squeeze.

"You okay, Sweetie?" She asked.

The girl dabbed at her eyes, then blew her nose and shook her head up and down. Then she shook it from side to side.

"It's really true. She walked from this house to St. Louis for him."

"Yes, she did. And back, too."

"In the middle of a war."

"Mmmm hmmm." The old woman sensed the girl sorting through it, wondering at it. She had herself. But she had recognized it, and she remembered how it felt. She rocked quietly and waited for the girl to continue.

"She must have loved him. I mean *really*." The girl spoke slowly, still deep in thought, not yet back from that time and place. She dabbed her eyes again. "That is just so *intense*!"

"I think he must have loved her just as much, don't you?"

"Yeah. It just amazes me." The girl answered quietly. She rocked, still wrapped up in the story, trying to comprehend the sheer magnitude of such an undertaking at that time.

She thought of one reason after another why it couldn't or shouldn't be done, the dangers, the difficulties, and the odds against success or even finding the man alive. But the woman went anyway. A trip such as that made on sheer faith, love, and force of will. She thought of people she knew who professed love for each other but doubted that many could or would withstand such an ordeal. Nor did she feel that they would go to the same extremes for their love, expending such effort, taking such risks. Quite literally putting their very lives on the line. She even wondered uncomfortably about herself. She sensed there was more to it.

"Gramma?" She asked.

"What, Sweetie?"

"Do you really think there's anything to that soul thing she talked about? The connection?"

"I know there is." The old woman answered. She leaned her head back against the rocker with a satisfied smile, relaxing. The girl was getting it.

"Do you really believe that stuff about everyone having a soul mate? C'mon, really?" The girl sounded awfully cynical for her age, but the old woman knew it was a bluff. Camouflage for the sensitive soul.

"Connections, soul mates. Yes, Dear, I do. You just read proof of it; you couldn't tell it was real? But it's easy to settle for less. Social pressure, complacency, rationalizing, cynicism. Being self-centered. Just not believing. It's hard to find. Harder nowadays, I think. So many more distractions now, lots of clutter in life we're led to believe will make us happy." The old woman sighed. No, it wasn't easy, finding the connections, keeping them intact. But it was worth any effort it took.

"I don't know if instincts and convictions hold up so well against facts and figures. Logic. The real world." The girl answered, testing.

"Yeah, well, facts and figures can lie. Logic can fool you, too. Most people remembered in history ignored them, did what couldn't be done. And I'd like to see you tell those two they didn't live in the real world." The old woman countered.

"Point. You're not going to let me off the hook, are you?" The girl looked at the old lady seriously, open to her, trusting.

"You do catch on." The old woman gave the girl a smile. "I guess it all depends on what you believe is most important in life."

"Like maybe to live it well?" The girl smiled back.

"Instincts, convictions, connections and all. And that's where happiness comes in, from living it well. You feel it when it's right. You know it. From the inside. Amazing how it all falls together, isn't it?" The old woman asked.

"You make it sound so simple."

"I didn't mean to, it's not. You have to give yourself, right down to your soul. And how many people would you trust with that? But it fulfills you like nothing else."

"Yeah." The girl said softly. "Screw the facts and figures. And all the clutter."

The old woman laughed out loud. "Well, most of it. And those stupid opinion polls, too!"

They rocked in comfortable silence for a few minutes. It was almost dark now and the light from the open windows shone out on them. The crickets started to chirp as a full moon rose slowly in the east. A whippoorwill called from the fencerow.

"Gramma…"

"Yes?"

"They danced right here on this porch. It really happened. It was real." Her voice was just above a whisper. The girl shook her head again.

"I know. It captivated me, too." The old woman answered softly.

"But she died, Gramma. After all that."

"Of course she died. She'd be almost two hundred if she hadn't."

"Gramma! You know what I mean! She went through all that then she dies."

"I know. I was curious, so I checked. She died in October of '66, almost two years later. Figures, she was a fighter. They're buried at the Baptist church, you know. I walked down and saw their stones. She'd just turned thirty-one, he lived to sixty. Never married again that I could tell."

"Really? All that time there and I never knew. I'm going to go see them. Not even two years, though. How sad." The girl shook her head again.

"Don't do that." The old woman warned.

"What?"

"Write it off as a sad story. That trivializes it, diminishes her. Just because she died young doesn't mean it wasn't as important and full a life as someone older. Don't you think she was truly happy?" The old woman questioned.

"Well, yes, once she found him again. But it doesn't seem fair."

"I'm sure she thought so, too. But she was ready when it came."

"Do you really think so? At her age?" The girl wasn't so sure.

"I think death was more a part of life then. And there was a war on. She saw it. We've tried to sanitize and separate death from life and not think about it. We take a long life for granted, we're seldom ready. But I think they made the most of their second chance. For what little time they had left I'm sure you could even stretch the imagination enough to say that they lived happily ever after. That's what you really want to hear."

"Those are the ones I like." She said softly.

"Don't we all, Sweetie." The old woman added ruefully.

"But this one I believe."

"Good. I'm glad you do."

They rocked in the spring night, thinking of the others who had rocked on the same porch so long ago. They wondered at how their lives had been enriched and inspired by the love of two people, long dead and forgotten, who had shared the same space in a different time. The feeling was magical, but palpably real. The old woman closed her eyes and listened to the sound of the chairs rocking together. The girl took in the spring night, felt its softness on her skin and smelled its new promise. In the moonlight she could almost swear she heard soft singing and saw movement in the periphery of her vision. Both felt the continuity that exists even through change, and were somehow comforted to know it was there. Time is fleeting; time is eternal.

They both saw the set of headlights approaching, and watched as they slowed, then turned up the long drive.

"He's here." The girl stated the obvious.

"Okay." The old woman came back to the moment only with great effort, reluctantly. "Dinner's ready and warming in the oven. You hungry?"

"Gramma?" The girl's voice was distant.

"Yes?"

"Would you mind holding dinner a bit? I've got to talk to him." She was still a long way off.

"Sure, Sweetie. Just come in when you're ready." The old woman rose and smoothed her sweater. She walked a little stiffly to the door and opened it.

"Gramma..." The girl was back now, vitally so. She turned and smiled affectionately at the old woman. There was more than a hint of mischief in that smile.

"What?" The old woman paused, holding the door, and turned back to the girl. She looked strong and confident, and the old woman could almost swear that she had a glow about her. The old woman smiled back at her warmly, feeling the involuntary catch in her throat. It still amazed her at times how much she loved that girl.

"I'll tell you what. You're not going anywhere after all, so why don't you give Jake a call when you go in? We'll be needing to get that garden turned..."

Author's Note

Rebecca's story captivated me from the time my late mother-in-law, Alma Nelle Moffatt Rynearson, first told it to me. Though many of the details are from my imagination, Augustus and Rebecca, Charles and Alma, Joseph and Belle were very real people. Augustus and Rebecca were Alma's paternal great grandparents. They lived near Troy, Tennessee, in Obion County.

The main events of the story were the details Alma recounted to me. Even the story-within-the-story of the bonnet box is true. That bonnet box is still in the family five generations later. The drawing of the box is an accurate depiction.

I knew from the time I first heard the story that I wanted to write it. My main concern was to do Rebecca's story justice. When I finally sat down to start it, I even wrote her letters out longhand, as she would have, before I typed them.

I have always identified very strongly with this particular time period in American history, and researching and writing this story have been among the more memorable experiences of my life.

Now I am sharing the story with you.

Roberta Nee Adams